SPALDING.

Youth league BASKETBALL

Coaching and Playing

JOE WILLIAMS & STAN WILSON

MASTERS PRESS

NTC/Contemporary Publishing Group

Library of Congress Cataloging-in-Publication Data

Williams, Joe.
    Youth league basketball: coaching and playing / Joe Williams and
Stan Wilson.
       p.   cm. — (Spalding sports library)
     ISBN 0-940279-70-3
     1. Youth league basketball.   2. Youth league basketball—Coaching.
I. Wilson, Stan.   II. Title.   III. Series.
GV886.3.W55   1993
796.323'62—dc20   93-5033
                                            CIP

Front cover photo of Vern Fleming, Jr. by Stephen Baker
Background photo provided by the Indiana Pacers
Cover design by Michele Holden

A Masters Press book
Published by Contemporary Books
A division of NTC/Contemporary Publishing Group, Inc.
4255 West Touhy Avenue, Lincolnwood (Chicago), Illinois 60646-1975 U.S.A.
Copyright © 1988 by The Athletic Institute, renewed by Masters Press
Printed in the United States of America
International Standard Book Number: 0-940279-70-3

20   19   18   17   16   15   14   13   12   11   10   9   8   7   6

The Better Sports for Kids Program

The Better Sports for Kids program is the proud mission of the National Youth Sports Coaches Association (NYSCA) which was created in 1981 to help improve out-of-school sports for over 20 million youth under the age of 16.

The non-profit association's staff of professionals work to implement a variety of programs, all in cooperation with national, state, and local associations.

The Better Sports for Kids program and its wide range of services help parents and kids get the most out of their participation in youth sports through programs such as the National Youth Sports Coaches Association national certification program for coaches, the National Association of Youth Leagues which helps leagues with all their needs in running a youth league organization, the All-American Drug-Free Team program which joins coaches and players in a drug education and prevention program, and the early introduction to lifetime sports through programs such as Hook a Kid on Golf.

The NYSCA is pleased to endorse the Spalding Youth League Series as an informative selection of coaching materials for youth coaches who wish to provide quality instruction and promote self esteem on and off the playing field.

NYSCA
National Youth Sports
Coaches Association

Table of Contents

YOUTH LEAGUE BASKETBALL
PLAYING AND COACHING

Foreword

Purpose

Every year volunteer coaches accept the responsibilities of guiding and teaching a team of young men or women for a season of basketball, and these responsibilities can be awesome. They range from teaching techniques to employing strategy to serving as a counselor and role model for a developing human being. The coach is a privileged person for he or she has the opportunity to make an immeasurable positive contribution to the life of a youth.

The hope behind this book is that all coaches, beginning and experienced alike, will find here clear and useful advice to help their players achieve and improve and play the sport of basketball. This book is written in honor of those players and in hope that they might grow physically, mentally, and spiritually because of the influence of their coaches.

The drills and techniques taught here are adequate for a wide range of players. They are the same skills that college, high school, middle school, and beginning players must master in order to play the game. Thus, it is our hope that this book will be helpful for every volunteer coach, from the one teaching a beginner to dribble, to the coach teaching high school players an offensive strategy. We have begun to use these methods in our church basketball program, and we are expecting great improvements as players are exposed year after year to consistent quality instruction.

May all who read this book and accept the responsibilities and privileges of coaching youth find in their volunteer jobs a world of success and joy.

Philosophy

If I could use one word to describe my basketball coaching philosophy, it would be unselfishness.

We teach our players to constantly be watching for the scoring play when they have the ball. While always looking for an open man, a player may continue toward the basket and try to score when no opponent picks him up.

A one-on-one player who does not pass the ball is a detriment to his coach and to his teammates. In fact, no one will want him on his team. But if you have an outstanding player and you can work on his moves and improve his self-image as a shooter, you will have an even better player. The bond between coach and player will become stronger as he gains from the experience and his talents become more useful in your offense.

The best one-on-one players are usually the best passers and they will lead your team in assists.

Like many other coaches, I also stress hard work and movement without the basketball. A player may not realize that in a typical game, he may have his hands on the ball only one-tenth of the time. (That's just four minutes in a college game of forty minutes and just over three minutes in a high school game, which lasts thirty-two minutes.)

We ask our players to think about what they are doing to help us win the game for the nine-tenths of the time when they don't have the ball. It is as important to be a good passer, a good defensive player, to rebound well and to keep your man off the boards, as it is to be a good shooter.

Half of the game is spent on defense and each player may handle the ball only about one-fifth of the offensive time. What he does without the ball is very important in contributing to a victory. Many times a ball is lost to the opposing team because the receiver did not get open to take a pass. He has to learn to move without the ball to be able to get open to receive the ball.

It is a good idea in pick-up games for players to work on different elements of their games, such as defense, rebounding and passing, instead of wasting time out on the floor by just standing around without the ball. This is an excellent way to develop better habits which can be used during a game to help your team win.

Again, let me emphasize--we always stress unselfishness.

Joe Williams
Stan Wilson

INTRODUCTION

Youth Sports: Benefits and Responsibilities for the Athlete and Coach

Benefits of Participating in Sports

Sports for children have become so popular that an estimated 20 million American children between the ages of six and sixteen play one or more sports each year. This tremendous interest suggests that parents and children believe that competitive athletics contribute positively to children's development. Such a wholesale endorsement may be misleading, however, unless it is counterbalanced by the sobering statistic that approximately 70 percent of the children drop out of organized sports programs by age fifteen. Many of the children who drop out are the ones who could benefit most from organized sports if directed by competent coaches. Thus, every coach, parent and athlete should answer the questions, "What are the benefits of competitive sports for children?" and "How can I be sure that these benefits are available to all children who participate in youth sports?"

Clearly, sports can have both positive and negative effects on children, but positive results can occur only if coaches and athletes conduct themselves in responsible ways. Although many of the benefits are immediately detectable and of a short-term nature, the most sought-after and important contributions of sports to total development are those that last far beyond the athlete's playing days.

In order for the benefits of sports to be available for all children, they must be identified, valued and included in their practices and games. Following are some of the benefits that are most commonly associated with children's sports participation:

- developing various sports skills
- learning how to cooperate and compete

- developing a sense of achievement, which leads to a positive self image
- developing an interest in and a desire to continue participation in sports during adulthood
- developing independence
- developing social skills
- learning to understand and express emotion, imagination, and appreciation for what the body can do
- developing speed, strength, endurance, coordination, flexibility, and agility
- developing leadership skills
- learning to make decisions and accept responsibilities

The Role of the Coach in Youth Sports

The coach of young athletes is the single most important adult in all of children's athletics. Other adults, such as officials and administrators, have important responsibilities, too, but no task is as important as that of the coach, who must guide young children physically, socially and emotionally as they grow from childhood through adolescence into adulthood.

The youth sports coach is required to play many roles. Most prominent among these are being a teacher and an instructor of skills, a friend who listens and offers advice, a substitute parent when the athlete's mother or father is not available or accessible, a medical advisor who knows when and when not to administer first aid and emergency care, a disciplinarian who rewards and corrects behavior, and a cheerleader who provides encouragement when everything goes wrong.

The age and development level of the athletes will determine how frequently the coach is asked to assume the various roles. Indeed, coaches may find themselves switching roles minute by minute as the fast-moving, complex nature of a contest calls for different responsibilities. The coach's responsibilities in each of the most common roles are discussed in the following sections.

The Coach As a Teacher

Although all of the coach's responsibilities are important, none is more important than being a good teacher. No matter how adept a coach is in other roles, these successes cannot overcome the harm caused by bad teaching. What then, are the characteristics of a good teacher?

Good teachers know what they are attempting to teach and are able to **select appropriate content** for the various levels of ability of their team members. Good teachers are **well organized,** both for the long-term season and in their daily practice and game plans. Good teacher are also **interested in the progress** of all their team members, including those who are inept and slow-learning. In summary, good teachers must love their athletes and their sport so much that practice sessions and games are joyful experiences for coaches and athletes.

The Coach As a Friend

Children play sports for many reasons, but one of the most frequently cited is that they like to be with friends and make new friends. Often, the most important role of the coach is just being a friend to a child who has none.

Being a friend to a friendless child often requires initiative and extra work for a coach, because such children are often unskilled and may have personality characteristics which make it difficult for other children to like them. Often the attention and affection by a coach is a sufficient stimulus for other team members to become more accepting, too. Regardless of the effort required, the coach must ensure that every child feels accepted as a member of the team.

The coach as a friend must be enthusiastic about sports and the participation of all children. Good friends are motivators who reward players with compliments and positive instruction instead of concentrating on errors. Good friends make children feel good about playing sports.

The Coach As a Substitute Parent

Nearly 50 percent of today's young athletes are likely to live in single-parent families. Whether or not coaches want the role of being a substitute parent, they are likely to acquire it. Even those children who live with both parents are apt to need the advice of their coach occasionally.

One of the most useful functions of the coach as a substitute parent is simply to listen to the child's problems. Frequently, the mere presence of an adult listener who inserts an occasional question to assist the child in clarifying the problem is all that is needed. As a coach, you must be careful not to judge the appropriateness of a parent's actions. In most instances the problems between parents and children are simply misunderstandings about children's desires and responsibilities. Such misunderstandings can usually be resolved by discussion, persuasion and compromise. However, in situations where parental actions are resulting in physical or mental abuse, the coach should contact professional counselors who are equipped to deal with such problems.

The Coach As Medical Advisor

Medical problems should be left to medical personnel who are equipped to deal with them. However, as a coach you are usually the first person at the scene of a youth sports injury and, therefore, are obligated to provide or obtain the necessary first aid. In addition, your judgment is likely to be called upon in situations where an injury has occurred and a decision must be made about whether the athlete should return to practice or competition.

A prudent policy for you is to resist making decisions which others are more qualified to make. You should seek the advice of medical personnel when injuries occur. Encourage your athletes to report aches, pains and injuries that are likely to impede their performance. Despite the emphasis on short-term objectives, your job is to safeguard the health of the athletes so that they are able to participate fully in physical activity well beyond the childhood years.

The Coach As Disciplinarian

One of the most frequently cited values of youth sports is their alleged contribution to the behavior and moral development of athletes. However, there are instances in children's sports where coaches and athletes have behaved in socially unacceptable ways. Obviously, attitudes and behaviors can be affected both positively and negatively in sports.

The first step to being a good disciplinarian is to establish the rules that will govern the athletes' behavior. These rules are more likely to be accepted and followed if the athletes have a voice in identifying them. Secondly, you must administer the rules fairly to all athletes. Desirable behavior must be enforced and undesirable actions must be corrected.

The Coach As a Cheerleader

Young athletes are likely to make numerous mental and physical errors as they attempt to learn specific skills. For that reason, their coaches must be tolerant of mistakes and eager to applaud any actions that represent improvement in performance.

Young athletes respond well to praise that is earned and given sincerely. Conversely, they are not very tolerant of criticism, especially when it occurs in association with a coach's expectations that are beyond their capacities or abilities. You must know your athletes so well that your requests are likely to result in a high ratio of successes to failures. When you choose tasks that are challenging but are likely to be done successfully you are in a position to be a **positive coach.** Positive coaches are likely to have fewer discipline problems than coaches who expect too much and then focus on inappropriate behavior. Being a positive coach is a good way to build the self-esteem that all young athletes need in order to feel successful about their sports participation.

The Role of the Athlete

A successful youth sports experience places demands on athletes as well as coaches. These responsibilites should be stated so that athletes and their parents understand what is expected of them. Some of the most important responsibilities of athletes are as follows:

- treat all teammates and opponents with respect and dignity
- obey all team and league rules
- give undivided attention to instruction of techniques, skills and drills
- always practice and play with a clear mind
- report all injuries to the coach for further medical evaluation
- discourage rule violations by teammates or opponents
- play under emotional control at all times
- avoid aggressive acts of self-destruction
- compliment good performances of teammates and opponents
- return to play when an injury is completely rehabilitated

Summary

Youth sports are designed to provide benefits to both athletes and coaches. However, these benefits cannot be obtained in the absence of clearly defined responsibilities. When both coaches and athletes accept and carry out the responsibilities defined in this introduction to Youth League Basketball, then the benefits of youth sports participation are likely to be realized.

Vern Seefeldt, Ph.D.
Director
Youth Sports Institute
Michigan State University

I. The First Phase of Basketball

Three skills that are absolutely essential in the execution of any offensive moves and strategies in basketball are the lay-up, dribbling, and passing. These skills are so basic, in fact, that many older players assume that they have mastered them and try to move on to practice more complicated offensive moves. No matter how old or experienced you are, however, you can greatly improve your game by emphasizing these basic skills. Included in the following pages are tips, drills, and instructions that players from the first grade through the college level could use. Be sure to spend plenty of time on these fundamentals because they will make all the difference in the execution of the offensive strategies employed later!

The Lay-Up

The lay-up is probably the most basic shot in basketball. It is a very natural move for an advanced player, but it can be extremely awkward for the beginner. Young players, particularly, find themselves struggling not only with the rhythm of the shot, but also with getting the ball to the basket.

To achieve the shooting position for a right-handed lay-up, shift your weight to and extend your left foot, explode off that foot, and then drive your right leg upward. The opposite is true for a left-handed lay-up: the right leg is extended, and the left leg is lifted. The inside foot is always the extended foot, so that a lay-up from the right side begins from the left foot, and a lay-up from the left side begins from the right foot. When the inside foot goes to the floor to push off, the outside knee comes up as high as possible.

During the drive upward, carry the ball in both hands to a point above and in front of your head. For a right lay-up, the left elbow protects the ball from the defender while the left hand balances the ball. The ball is released to the shooting hand, and the shooting arm is extended fully. The right hand (with the elbow in and the triceps parallel with the floor) bends at the wrist and with the fingers pushes the ball toward the goal. The wrist action is similar to the dribbling action which will be taught later. The palm of the shooting hand should face the basket while the ball is controlled with the fingertips.

When shooting a lay-up, keep your head up and your eyes focused at a point on the backboard where the ball is to be banked into the basket. At the release, place the ball gently against the backboard, and on the follow-through snap your wrist inward so that your fingers are pointing toward the basket.

1-1A The Lay-Up
Head up, right elbow in, left foot planted.

1-1B The Lay-Up
Explode off the left foot, and extend the right hand.

Drills

1. Players form one line for lay-ups with the coach passing the ball.
2. Players start from half-court and dribble all the way to the basket for a lay-up.
3. Players form two lines, one of shooters and one of rebounders. (This drill uses feeding, rebounding, and passing.)

Coaching Tips

1. Explain to the beginning player exactly what you expect of him in shooting a lay-up.
2. To teach the lay-up the coach must try to help the player develop a regular rhythm of shooting. As you call out the words "One, two, and up" or "Left, right, and up," the player can begin to develop the rhythm necessary for this shot.

3. As you say "Left, and up," make sure that the player's right arm and right foot go up simultaneously.

4. A coach who persists with patience and understanding can make a lifelong friend of the beginning player who struggles with and finally masters the lay-up. Equally, a coach can give a lifelong gift to more advanced players by helping them learn how to shoot a lay-up correctly from their weak hand side.

Dribbling

Ball-handling separates the good basketball players from the mediocre ones. Here, particularly, it is important for beginning players to learn correct fundamentals and for more advanced players to work on correcting bad habits. Good habits such as looking up instead of at the ball, using only the hand, wrist and lower arm to maneuver the ball, and keeping the ball at an appropriate height while dribbling do not come naturally. When they are developed and reinforced by the coach year after year, these are the habits that make good ball-handlers and successful players.

In the following sections the techniques for proper dribbling will be presented. Learning the basic control dribble may be quite a hard task for a younger player, but the more advanced can be challenged by learning the techniques for the "crossover change" (a change of direction), or the methods for the "speed dribble" (dribbling while running).

Basic Dribble Position

A ready position, or basic offensive stance, is fundamental to executing both the control and speed dribbles. In this position, your head is up and your knees are slightly flexed, so that your body is in a semi-crouched position. Your eyes focus down the floor in front of you. The degree of body crouch varies according to the speed of the dribble and the conditions under which you are dribbling.

Your finger and thumb tips contact the ball; the palm of the hand does not. Your hand is positioned at the top of the ball toward the back half of the top surface.

Control Dribble

You should begin by bouncing the ball slightly forward, using fingertip control. Fingertip control is executed by flexing the wrist and fingers. Your lower arm from the elbow to fingertips moves in a pumping action to project, receive, and then project the ball again.

If you dribble the ball at sock- to knee-high, you gain better control and reduce the opponent's chance of stealing it. Again, the ball is protected with the arm and leg nearest your opponent.

1-2 Basic Dribble Position
Head up; eyes focused ahead, knees flexed, ball contacted with fingers and thumb tips, free arm out for ball protection.

1-3 Dribble Options
As you approach the defender with the ball, you have three good options for getting past: the crossover change, the speed dribble, and the hesitate and drive.

Coaching Tips

1. Work to help the player develop the rhythm of using the elbow, then the wrist, then the fingers. Bad habits develop from using the entire arm and the shoulder in the motion of dribbling.

2. Sock-high dribbling dramatically decreases the changes of the opponent stealing the ball. Although it may seem too low for your players, practicing dribbling from this height will be a tremendous advantage for them in the future.

Crossover Change Techniques

After learning the control dribble, the player can develop methods of changing direction while dribbling. The crossover change is illustrated in the following pictures, and it is particularly useful for getting by an opponent. Players who obviously dribble with only one hand are easy to stop, but players who can cross over their dribble can often gain an advantage over a defender.

Execute the crossover change by bouncing the ball to your opposite hand. Make sure to keep your shoulders square to the direction of travel. As you are moving past the defender, drive off the trailing leg and protect the ball with the free hand, arm and leg nearest your opponent.

1-4A Crossover Change
Stop on foot opposite dribbling hand (allows you to have three options of crossover change, speed dribble, or hesitate and drive).

1-4B Crossover Change
Drive off the trailing leg, and bounce the ball sharply to your opposite hand.

1-4C Crossover Change
Exchange must be made quickly since the ball will be exposed to your opponent.

Speed Dribble

A speed dribble is made in an effort to pass a defender in a high speed drive down court or to the basket. It can be a most effective method of getting open, but certainly adjustments need to be made to execute the speed dribble properly.

As the ball is dribbled at speed, the body leans more forward and into the dribble. The ball is controlled from knee to chest level.

Keep your shoulders square to the direction of travel while protecting the ball with your arm and leg.

1-5A The Speed Dribble
From the basic dribble position, lean forward and into the ball.

1-5B The Speed Dribble
Protect the ball with your arm and leg and control it from waist to chest high.

Hesitate and Drive

Some people call this move "pulling the string." As you approach the defensive player, hesitate slightly, lift your head, and then explode off the trailing foot. This move is used when you determine that the crossover change is not needed in getting past a defender. It is best used in conjunction with the crossover change so that the defender will never know which way you are going.

1-6A Hesitate and Drive
Drive to the defender and hesitate on foot opposite dribbling hand.

1-6B Hesitate and Drive
Initiate drive past defender with the right leg.

Dribbling Drills

1. Have the players kneel and dribble with their eyes closed to get the feel of the ball.

1-7 Dribbling Drill
Practice dribbling on your knees with your eyes closed; concentrate on keeping the ball low.

2. Practice the control dribble by having the players dribble half court, down with their right hand and back with their left hand. Emphasize that they look down court and not at the ball, and try to get them to dribble sock- to knee-high.

3. "The Zig-Zag Dribble:" To work on the crossover dribble, have the players dribble to the right with the right hand for 5 to 15 feet, then drive to the left with the left hand for 5 to 15 feet, crossover back to right for the same distance, and then back to the left, etc.

4. Hesitate–and–drive drills: Have each player drive across the half-court line with the defense man guarding at the line. They can either crossover to drive the free throw area for a pull-up jump shot, or hesitate and drive past their opponent for a pull-up jump shot on the wing. Practice this with the right hand on the right side of the court and with the left hand on the left side of the court. (See Diagram 1.)

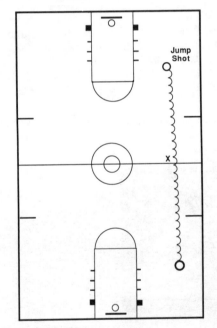

Diagram 1

(Legend for Diagrams is in Appendix.)

Dribbling Coaching Tip

Teach the player how to use the crossover dribble and the hesitation drive in conjunction with each other so that as the player approaches a defensive player, he can drive either direction depending upon the reaction of the defense.

Passing

Although passing the ball may seem like a naturally acquired skill, many players get into bad habits of sloppy passing. Time spent practicing passing will help younger players avoid these habits and give more experienced players a chance to sharpen up their game.

Chest Pass Techniques

The chest pass is made from a ready position, i.e., facing the target with knees flexed, head up, and eyes on the intended receiver.

Hold the ball at chest level with your hands placed above and slightly behind the ball's center and your elbows bent. Grip the ball with your fingers and thumbs, keeping the palms of your hands off the ball.

1-8A Chest Pass
Start from ready position—head up, eyes on receiver, ball at chest level.

1-8B Chest Pass
Step to the target and release the ball; pronate wrists inward with thumbs down upon release.

Two-Handed Bounce Pass

The two-handed bounce pass is merely a variation of the chest pass, in that the ball is thrown on one bounce to the teammate.

Apply all the chest pass techniques to project the ball on one bounce to your teammate. Avoid "telegraphing" the pass.

One-Handed Flip Pass

This pass is sometimes referred to as a "hook pass" because such a pass is very often effective in getting the ball around a closely guarding defender. Like the chest pass, the one-handed flip pass may be delivered on a level trajectory or made to bounce once to a teammate. Often the bounce pass is the safer pass to make.

From the **ready position**, step out to the side of the defender where you intend to release the pass. With your eyes on the receiver, grip the ball firmly in both hands until the point of release. Project the ball with the outside hand and pronate the wrist over the top of the ball to release it with a "flipping action."

Overhead Pass Techniques

The overhead pass is also executed from a **ready position**, which means you should face the target with your head up, keep your eyes on the receiver, and grip the ball with your fingertips. (Often, such a pass is made after a pivot to achieve a ready position.)

From the position, extend your arms upward, with the ball above and slightly in front of your head. The proper movement in an

1-9 Overhead Pass
Head up, facing target, ball overhead—step to the receiver and follow through with arms and wrists.

overhead pass is to step toward the target and simultaneously bend the wrists as if to cock the ball. Extend the elbows and uncock the wrist as you release the ball so that your wrists are rotated inward and the thumbs pointed down. The pass should be received at approximately chest height.

Baseball Pass Techniques

A baseball pass may be thrown farther than any other pass; however, if the pass is not made properly and under the right circumstances, control and accuracy may be sacrificed. To throw this pass, draw the ball over your throwing shoulder and behind your ear. Extend your free arm toward the receiver while stepping out with the forward foot.

The ball is thrust forward while your weight is transferred from your back foot to the forward foot. Release the ball at full arm extension as the leg on the throwing side comes forward to achieve a balanced follow-through. Note that the release is executed through fingertip control and wrist snap.

Keep the free hand up and in front of you until the point of release in case you decide to control the ball rather than throw the pass.

1-10A Baseball Pass
Draw ball over throwing shoulder and behind the ear. Keep opposite hand up in case you stop the pass.

1-10B Baseball Pass
Fingertip control and wrist snap are essential elements for an effective pass.

Passing Drills

Practice passing as intently as you might practice shooting. Form the players into two lines and practice the chest pass, the overhead pass, and the baseball pass. If you emphasize strengthening the wrists, you will develop passers who can pass accurately down the length of the court with a chest pass.

Passing Coaching Tips

1. A good pass is the result of a sharp and complete motion. It begins with a step toward the target and a simultaneous push of the ball with the arms. At the release of the ball, emphasize the proper movement of the wrists and hands: they should rotate so that the palms are facing out and the thumbs are pointing down. It is important to keep the trajectory of the ball on a level plane.

2. The passer should work on passing away from the defender, but the receiver also has the responsibilities of working hard to get open and working hard to catch the ball. Many difficult passes can still be caught by a good receiver.

Drills That Combine the Lay-Up, Dribbling, and Passing

A Combination Drill:

Diagram 2A shows Player 1 under the basket. Player 1 should dribble out past the top of the circle and pass to Player 2, who is on this side of the half-court line. Player 2 should dribble for the lay-up, and Player 1 should trail him. Diagram 2B shows Player 1 cutting out to the half-court line on the opposite side. Player 2 should get his own rebound and dribble out to pass to Player 1, who will drive for the lay-up on the opposite end. This is an effective drill for combining all of the skills.

A 2-on-1 Drill

Players 1 and 2 pass back and forth as they drive down the court to the basket. As they approach the defender who is positioned just past the foul line, their moves are determined by the defender's moves. If the defender commits to the man with the ball, the man with the ball must pass to his partner. If the defender drops back to cover the pass, the man with the ball must go for the lay-up. This seems like a simple drill, but many players will force a shot when they are covered. It is important to learn to be unselfish and pass the ball when you are covered. (See Diagram 3.)

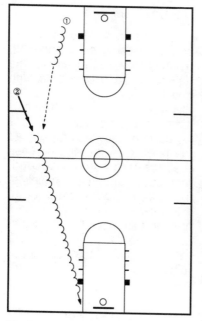

Diagram 2-A

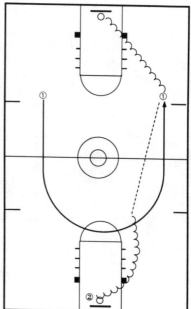

Diagram 2-B

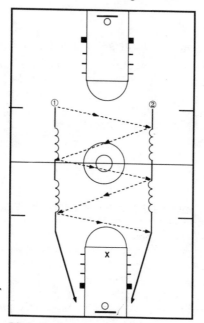

Diagram 3

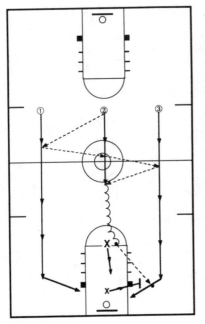

Diagram 4

A 3-on-2 Drill:

Diagram 4 shows three players passing back and forth as they drive down court. The defenders are in the middle, high and low. This drill teaches the players to pull up for the short jump shot rather than forcing a lay-up when they are covered. As the players on the outside pass the free-throw line extended, they cut in and to the baseline. The middle player stops short of the free-throw line either to shoot the short jump shot or to pass to one of his players. Again the moves of the offense are deter-mined by the moves of the defense.

(Legend for Diagrams is in Appendix.)

II. Fundamentals Of The Correct Shot

The Basic Shot

Regardless of the type of shot which will be taken, the basic offensive stance is the same. The upper arm is parallel to the floor and the forearm is bent at a 90 degree angle. The wrist is cocked with the shooting hand slightly under and behind the ball. In this position, your shoulder, elbow, hand, and ball should be lined up toward the target. It is especially important while keeping these parts of the arm in a lever position before taking a shot that you do not let your elbow get too far away laterally from the side of the body. A flying elbow changes the angle of the shot, and this can affect both aim and ball control.

The target is the middle of the basket, halfway between the front and back of the rim.

In shooting the ball, extend or straighten the arm toward the target, extend or flip the wrist forward and let the ball roll off your fingertips. When this technique is properly executed, the ball will have backspin rotation. Simply consider shooting as using a mechanical lever with all of the angles--shoulder, elbow, wrist, and ball--lined up toward the target.

Shooting Drill

A good drill procedure in practice is to have the players start with the hand under the ball, rotate so the wrist is cocked and the arm bent at a 90-degree angle, then extend toward the target, using only the forefinger to guide the ball toward the basket. This teaches ball control and gives the ball the right arc. (The one-finger shot should not be taken, of course, during a game.)

2-1A Fundamentals of the Correct Shot
For drill purposes start with your hand under the ball.

2-1B Fundamentals of the Correct Shot
Rotate the ball.

2-1C Fundamentals of the Correct Shot
Wrist cocked; shoulder, elbow, and wrist aligned; hand under and behind the ball.

2-1D Fundamentals of the Correct Shot
Extend your arm toward the target, and flip your wrist forward for proper rotation.

III. Offensive Moves From Shooting Position

Once you have learned how to dribble, pass, and shoot, you must begin to learn how to put those skills to use in offensive situations. Players with good skills can become easily frustrated when they get into live game situations and aren't able to apply what they know. The techniques that follow are not difficult once the basic techniques of dribbling and shooting have been learned. You simply need to understand how to perform them and to be able to practice them in game situations.

Basic to any offensive move is the skill of receiving the ball properly and moving into shooting position, so that is covered first in this chapter. We then present a method for driving to the basket, called the Long Step Drive, and explain the proper form for the jump shot. Finally, there are power moves, methods for shooting from inside which are very effective when the lay-up has been stopped close to the basket.

The moves we show here are the moves that work, and a young person who will practice them moves on his own until they become natural will likely prove to be a formidable basketball player.

Coaching Tips

1. Show these moves to your players, allow them to be practiced in game situations, and encourage the players to practice the moves when they are shooting by themselves. Often players practice flamboyant, flashy shots that are actually impractical in real games.

2. A coach can be extremely helpful simply by showing his players the most effective ways of using their skills when they are covered by a whole team of defenders.

Receiving the Ball from a Teammate

The player who moves well without the ball and is constantly on the move most often gets free for a pass from a teammate.

Usually the most effective means of receiving a pass is to take a couple of steps toward the passer. In so doing the receiver reduces the distance and time which the defender has to intercept the ball. Faking toward the passer or to one side, then reversing in the opposite direction, also may provide an opportunity to receive a pass safely.

It is always important to keep your eye on the ball and to immediately set up in shooting position. This position allows you the option of shooting, passing, or dribbling and driving to the basket.

Coaching Tip

Help your players begin to think of those three options every time they receive the ball.

3-1A Receiving the Ball From a Teammate
Move to get clear for a pass from a teammate.

3-1B Receiving the Ball From a Teammate
Receive the ball and move into shooting position.

3-1C Receiving the Ball From a Teammate
Proper shooting position gives the options of shooting, driving, or passing.

Drive from the Shooting Position

All drives to the basket start from the shooting or starting position. Upon moving to receive the ball from a teammate, the player must think in terms of the options of shooting, passing, or dribbling and driving. The first move discussed here is a long-step drive, with the intention of driving for an open lay-up.

The first step in the long step drive is with the right foot for a right-handed player. The player receives the ball and pivots on the left foot

3-2A Drive From the Shooting Position
If your left foot is the pivot foot, start the long-step drive with your right foot.

3-2B Drive From the Shooting Position
You must dribble before you pick up your pivot foot.

3-2C Drive From the Shooting Position
Drive to the basket for a lay-up if you are open.

to face the basket. The long step drive with the right foot is most effective then because the player can take a step with the right foot past the defender, and he doesn't have to dribble the ball until after he lifts his left or pivot foot from the ground.

More advanced players will determine which foot is their pivot foot by their location on the court, not by which hand is dominant. They will then take the long step drive with the opposite foot. It is helpful for beginning players to learn the long step drive by first practicing with their dominant hand.

Go to meet the ball, pivot to face the basket, and assume a starting position. Make a slight head fake upward as if to shoot, then pull the ball across your body and with the foot opposite the fake, explode with a drive step past the defender. The ball is protected forward and to the side of your dribbling hand. Simultaneously thrust your opposite or pivot foot forward to continue penetration of the drive. Protect the ball with your arm and leg nearest the defender.

Crossover Long-Step Drive

Any offensive player is ineffective if he can only drive to one side, and often beginning players are afraid to drive with the hand opposite their dominant hand. A little time spent at formal practices emphasiz-

3-3A Crossover Long-Step
Start from shooting position.

3-3B Crossover Long-Step
Pull Ball across body, and make a crossover step with the foot opposite the pivot foot.

3-3C Crossover Long-Step
Explode past the defender.

3-3D Crossover Long-Step
Continue to the basket for the lay-up.

ing the fundamentals of a drive with the opposite hand will help the players practice these moves on their own.

The crossover long step drive must begin from the shooting position! Your drive foot is again the foot opposite the pivot foot, and your step is in the opposite direction of the long step drive.

Go to meet the ball, pivot, and face the basket in shooting position. Pull the ball across your body, and make the crossover long step with your drive foot. Explode past the defender. As you thrust the ball forward and to the side of your dribbling hand, drive the opposite foot forward to continue penetration. Protect the ball against the defender with your arm and leg.

Jump Shot Techniques

The jump shot is made from a starting position, with head up, eyes on the basket, and your weight distributed on the balls of your feet. The foot on the side of your shooting hand is extended slightly.

During the jump and the shot, the ball is controlled by both hands. Place the hand opposite your shooting hand on the side and slightly behind the center of the ball. The shooting hand is placed behind the ball.

While exploding upward, carry the ball to the shooting position with both hands. The shooting arm forms a 90-degree angle, and your eyes will be focused on the basket.

Make the release when your shooting arm is at full extension and at the peak of your jump. On the release, control the shot with your fingertips and follow through by flipping your wrist forward.

3-4A Jump Shot Techniques
Ready position, facing basket with head up.

3-4B Jump Shot Techniques
Explode up with eyes on the rim. The shooting arm forms a 90 degree angle with the elbow close to the body.

Power Lay-Up

The power lay-up is an extension of the long-step drive technique and gives the offensive player three options as he looks for a scoring play in one-on-one situations: passing to an open man, going for the lay-up, or taking a jump shot after making a step-through move if stopped by a defender.

After a slight fake upward as if to take a long jump shot, the offensive player tenses his pivot leg slightly as he prepares to push off from the ball of his foot. He then takes a driving long step in the direction he wants to go. As he gains an advantage on the defender, the ball-handler pulls up in the basket area with both feet planted solidly in an attempt to get the defensive man on his back. (This contact may produce a three-point play.) If he makes a power move toward the basket, the player should keep the ball in good shooting position in case he has to reset his shot to avoid a block.

Keep your body under control at all times. Do not let your feet leave the ground until you actually take the shot.

3-5A The Power Lay-Up
The pivot leg tenses as you push off taking a drive step toward the basket.

3-5B The Power Lay-Up
After gaining an advantage on the defender, pull up in basket area with both feet planted.

3-5C The Power Lay-Up
Keep the ball in good shooting position at all times, and don't let your feet leave the ground until taking the shot.

IV. Offensive Moves From The High Post And Wing Positions

The following paragraphs describe four offensive moves that are effective from either the high post or outside wing positions. They are the Long-Step Drive to pull up for the short jump shot, the Step-Through Move after the Long-Step Drive, the Crossover Long-Step Drive for the short jump shot, and the Step-Through Move after the Crossover Long-Step Drive.

All of these drives and moves can be most effective when you find yourself in a one-on-one situation. The object is to get by the defender and get open for a short jump shot. If the jump shot is not open, the step-through option gives you another move to help you get an open shot.

Long-Step Drive, Pull-Up and Short Jump Shot

A forced shot rarely finds its target. Therefore, it is just as important to take a good shot near the basket as it is from farther

4-1A Long-Step Drive Pull-Up and Short Jump Shot
Start long-step drive.

4-1B Long-Step Drive Pull-Up and Short Jump Shot
Pull up and plant the inside foot.

4-1C Long-Step Drive Pull-Up and Short Jump Shot
Take the jump shot.

4-1D Long-Step Drive Pull-Up and Short Jump Shot
Point feet toward basket, keep body balance, and observe good shooting techniques.

away. And it is equally important not to develop a selfish attitude in looking for a scoring play.

If, in driving toward the basket, the offensive player finds he cannot continue because of the defense, he can either pull up and pass off to a teammate, or attempt a jump shot.

In taking the shot, plant the inside foot and go straight up with both feet pointed toward the basket, keeping body balance and good shooting technique in mind.

Step-Through Move

If the defense stops the basic jump shot, a quick step-through move often can be effective in getting the ball-handler open for a different type of shot. If this maneuver is also blocked, he can still step back and try again for the jump shot or pass off to a teammate.

The inside foot, or the one closest to the free throw lane, is the pivot foot. In a step-through move, your outside foot is moved quickly across the defender's feet in hopes of gaining an offensive advantage by getting the defender on your back.

Then, with your feet planted, re-establish your body balance by squatting and moving your head back. Move the ball through to the open shooting area if you can, keeping fundamental shooting techniques in mind at all times.

Keep your body under control and do not let your feet leave the ground until you take the short jump shot. Otherwise, you may get caught in mid air. As long as your pivot foot is still anchored, you can always step back if the short jump shot isn't available.

4-2A Step-Through Move
When the defense stops the jump shot, the step-through could be the next move.

4-2B Step-Through Move
With the pivot foot planted, step across the defender with the outside foot. Squat and move the head back to regain balance.

4-2C Step-Through Move
Do not leave your feet again unless you take the short jump shot.

Crossover Long-Step to Pull-Up Jump Shot

Go to meet the ball, pivot and face the basket in shooting position. Pull the ball across your body and make the crossover long step with the drive foot. Explode past the defender! As the ball is thrust forward and to the side of your dribbling hand, drive the opposite foot forward to continue penetration. Protect the ball against the defender with your arm and leg. Pull up, planting the outside foot to re-establish your balance and keeping both feet pointed toward basket. Come straight up for the jump shot, using basic shooting fundamentals with your shoulder, elbow, and hand lined up.

4-3A Crossover Long-Step to Pull-Up Jump Shot
Start from shooting position.

4-3B Crossover Long-Step to Pull-Up Jump Shot
Keep your arm and leg between the ball and the Defender.

4-3C Crossover Long-Step to Pull-Up Jump Shot
Pull up, get your balance.

4-3D Crossover Long-Step to Pull-Up Jump Shot
Go for the shot.

Step-Through Move After Crossover to Pull-Up Jump Shot

From a different camera angle and floor position, this photograph shows the step-through maneuver against a defender when the player pulls up but can't make a jump shot attempt.

The offensive player steps through, attempting to gain an advantage by having the defender on his back. From the step-through, the player with the ball can either shoot a short jump shot, or step back and attempt a longer jump shot, or pass off to a teammate.

4-4A Step-Through Move After the Crossover
The jump shot is stopped.

4-4B Step-Through Move After the Crossover
Shoulder and arm protect the ball from the defender.

4-4C Step-Through Move After the Crossover
Focus on the basket as you step through.

4-4D Step-Through Move After the Crossover
Take the short jump shot.

V. Skeleton Offensive Drills

This is a set of offensive drills that will help your team learn a simple and effective offensive plan. They involve four players. Players 1, 2, and 3 are perimeter players who work from different positions on the court, depending on the location of the ball and the movements of the other players. Player P is the post man, who will remain at the post, but will move to different positions on the post, depending on the position of the ball and the movement of the other players. (See Diagram 5.)

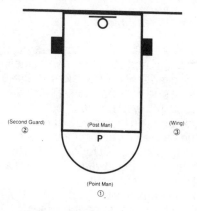

Diagram 5

The offense is designed to teach the players to receive the ball, get into shooting position, and either shoot a high percentage shot, pass to a player in a higher percentage scoring area, or drive to the basket. If a player drives to the basket, and cannot shoot a lay-up or pass to an open player, he must stop and use the moves discussed in the chapter "Offensive Moves from Shooting Position." Finally, if the step-through moves are not open, the player must pass back out to an open teammate to start the process over again. Here's the process:

The drill begins with one guard at the top of the key and two guards at either wing, roughly even with the foul line extended. The post man is at the "high" post position, but is in the center of the lane on the foul line. Player 1 at the top of the key has the ball and will pass to Player 2. In order to receive the ball Player 2 must get open, so he

must practice faking toward the basket and then coming back out to
receive the ball. (See Diagram 6.)

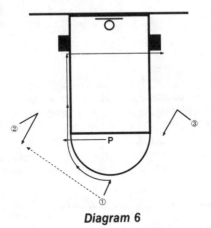

Diagram 6

When Player 1 passes the ball to Player 2, he (Player 1) immediately cuts to the basket, and the post man comes to the high post
position closest to Player 2. Player 3 fakes to the basket and then
comes out to Player 1's former position. Player 2 now has several
options. He can pass to Player 1, who is cutting toward the basket.
He can shoot if he is open. He can pass to the post man if he is open,
or he can drive to the basket. If none of these options is open, he can
continue the offense by passing out to Player 3, who is now at the top
of the key. Player 1, after driving toward the basket and not receiving
the ball, moves out to the former position of Player 3, so the offense is
now ready to begin over again with the perimeter players at different
positions. Diagram 7 illustrates these movements.

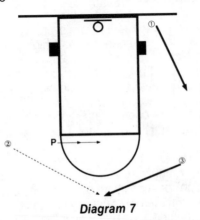

Diagram 7

The following diagrams will illustrate what each player should do when Player 2 takes an option other than passing to the open player 3. The goal of these drills and diagrams is to enable a team to maintain an organized offensive effort and to help players understand what they are supposed to be doing from any position on the court to make the offense work best.

In Diagram 8, Player 2 passes to the post man, who has come out to the high post position nearest him in a ready position to receive the ball. As soon as Player 2 passes the ball, he cuts toward the basket in hopes of receiving a back-door pass as his defender looks to the post man. Player 1 also cuts to the basket, and he crosses above Player 2, possibly having a pick set for him or setting a pick for Player 2. The post man receives the ball and faces the basket in shooting position ready for a jump shot or a one-on-one drive to the basket. He also looks to see if Players 1 or 2 are open. Notice that the players in Diagram 8 are in different positions than in Diagram 7. It is assumed in Diagram 8 that the drill has been run and Player 1 has already cut through to the opposite side of the floor.

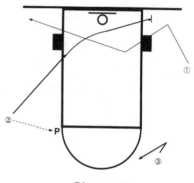

Diagram 8

Diagram 9 illustrates a variation of a pass to the post man. Player 2 drives to the foul line, and the post man makes a back-door cut to the basket. Player 2 then looks for the lob pass to the post man or pulls up for the jump shot or step-through move. If none of these options is available, Player 2 continues the offense by passing back to Player 3 at the top of the key. Player 2 could also skip the option of passing to player 3 and pass across to player 1, if he is not open. This would be called a "skip" pass.

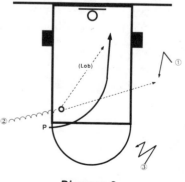

Diagram 9

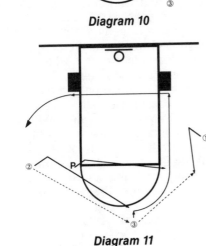

Diagram 10

In Diagram 10, Player 2 drives to the baseline. He again looks for the lob pass to the postman, who does a back-door cut to the basket on the opposite side from Player 2. If that pass is not open, Player 2 pulls up for the free jump shot or the step-through moves. If these are not open, he looks to Player 1 to be open for a jump shot, and then finally back to Player 3 to continue the offense.

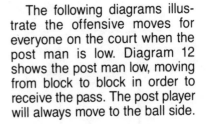

Diagram 11

In Diagram 11, Player 3 is now at the top of the key to set up the offense as usual. Players 1 and 2 are at the wing positions, and Player 3 can look to them as receivers to continue the skeleton offense drill.

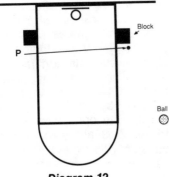

Diagram 12

The following diagrams illustrate the offensive moves for everyone on the court when the post man is low. Diagram 12 shows the post man low, moving from block to block in order to receive the pass. The post player will always move to the ball side.

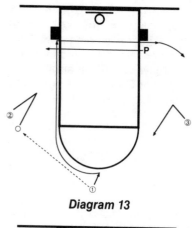

Diagram 13

Diagram 13 shows the post man away as the ball is passed to Player 2. The post player moves to the ball side, and as he moves, he may try to use Player 1 as a pick to get open. To do this he must cut immediately behind Player 1.

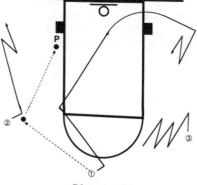

Diagram 14

In Diagram 14 Player 2 receives the pass, faces the basket in shooting position and, seeing P open, passes the ball to the low post. Player P will attempt to score, and if not open, will look to see which perimeter players have worked without the ball to get into an open passing lane for the short pop jump shot. If no one is open, then the perimeter players will set the offense and continue.

In Diagram 15 Player 2 has received the ball in shooting position. Player 1 has cut through

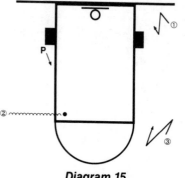

Diagram 15

to the opposite corner, and P is covered at the low post. Player 2 penetrates to the free-throw lane area looking for the pass to P (See Diagram 16A for an explanation of P's movements) or a pass to Player 1, who is trying to get into an open passing lane. Player 2 is also attempting to score on his own by driving to the basket or pulling up for the short jump shot or the step-through moves. If none of these options is open, the ball is passed to Player 3, and the offense continues.

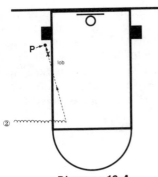

Diagram 16-A

Diagram 16A explains the movements of the post player. Here Player P is being fronted by his defensive player. In this situation Player 2 will attempt a lob pass over P's defender to create a possible power move opportunity for P.

Diagram 16-B

If Player P's defender drops off (Diagram 16B), P steps in front of his defender and is open to receive the pass directly from Player 2's drive to the lane area.

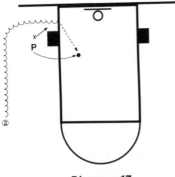

Diagram 17

Diagram 17 shows Player 2 driving the baseline and P moving to get open for the short jump shot if his man drops off or to pick up or help cover Player 2's drive to the basket. If Player 2 cannot score or pass to P, he looks to see if Player 1 is in an open passing lane. If not, the ball is passed to Player 3, who resets the offense.

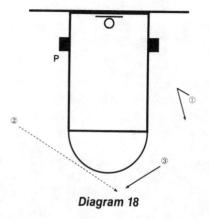

Diagram 18

Diagram 18 shows that Player 1 has passed to Player 2 and cut through to the opposite corner. Player 2 has not found P open, nor has he found an opportunity to shoot or drive. He then passes the ball to Player 3 at the top of the key where Player 3 will reset the offense by passing to either Player 1 or Player 2 and then cutting to the basket. The offense continues.

Coaching Tip

Continually remind the players to look for the pass to the player who has the highest percentage scoring opportunity. Also discourage any forced shots! It is just as bad to force a shot from two feet away as it is to force a shot from 20 feet. A forced shot encourages selfishness and is detrimental to team play.

(Legend for Diagrams is in Appendix.)

VI. Half Court Offense

There is no one offense that is the best offense. There are almost as many offenses as there are coaches, and if there were "one great offense," then all coaches would employ it. Each coach will want to devise his own offense which will best utilize the fundamentals that are used in his practices.

The following offense is designed to take advantage of unselfish one-on-one scoring moves. Almost any time a player receives the ball away from the basket area, he should face the basket in shooting position, looking to see if there is a player open closer to the basket, looking to see if he himself is open for an easy shot, or looking to see if he has an opportunity to drive toward the basket utilizing his scoring opportunities through passing, power lay-ups, pull-up jump shots, or step-through moves.

The Penetration Offense

The penetration offense uses three players on the perimeter. Player 1 is the ball handling guard, quarterback, or point guard. Player 2 is the second guard, shooting guard, or big guard. Player 3 is the shooting forward, wing man, or small forward. The perimeter players are all interchangeable in the half-court penetration offense. The designations 1, 2 and 3 are used to follow their progression in the half-court offense, and their differences are more apparent in their full court offensive and defensive assignments.

The two post players will be designated either high post (HP) or low post (LP), and they can also be interchanged. The low post player should have a good scoring touch around the basket, be the tallest and biggest player, and be able to catch and pass the ball well. The high post player should have a good scoring touch on the jump shot from the free throw line, be an excellent passer, and jump well. He should have the ability to catch the ball in mid air and score. As this player gains greater physical ability, he will be able to dunk the basketball.

This offense, a continuation of the skeleton offensive drill that we have been practicing, integrates into a pattern the complementary interrelationships of the different players' offensive moves.

Diagrams 19-A, B, C

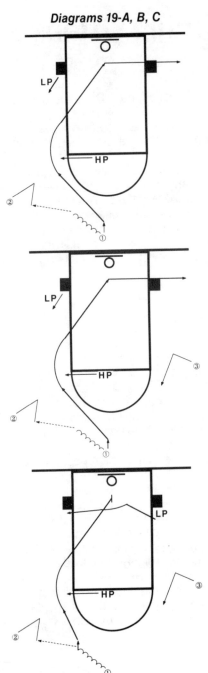

In Diagram 19A, Player 1 passes to Player 2 who faked inside to free himself from his defensive man and then moved up to receive the open pass from 1. Player 1 cuts through to the ball side of the high post player, and as soon as he gets to the free-throw line extended, he cuts to the basket. The HP moves to the free throw line on the ball side and Player 3 fakes inside and gets himself open to be a receiver. (If Player 1's defender plays on the ball side, Player 1 will be open for a lob. Be sure to pay close attention to player 1's movements as this can be a very effective play.)

In Diagram 19B, the low post player was away from the ball on the entry pass from Player 1 to Player 2. As Player 2 receives the ball, the low post moves to the side of the ball and positions himself on the block. The high post, on the free-throw line, moves to the side of the ball. Player 1 cuts through and tries to obstruct the high post's man, then cuts directly to the opposite side of the basket. If his opponent stays ball side, Player 1 may be open for a lob pass in the scoring area. Player 3, after faking inside, moves toward the top of the circle, staying in an open passing lane. (See Diagram 19-C)

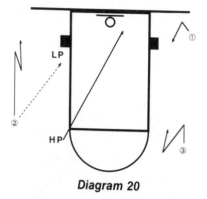

Diagram 20

In Diagram 20, Player 2 passes the ball to the low post man and then moves to stay in an open passing lane ready to receive an outlet pass should his man drop down to help on the low post. LP looks for HP cutting to the basket, or any of the perimeter players who might be open.

In Diagram 21, the ball is passed to HP at the high post. LP positions himself to receive the pass from HP or maintain an offensive rebounding position. HP looks to see if LP is open, or if he has open jump shot from the free throw line. He also may drive to the basket. If none of these options is open, HP looks for the pass to the perimeter player in the best scoring position.

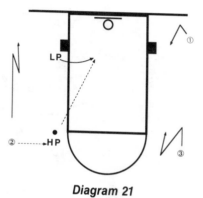

Diagram 21

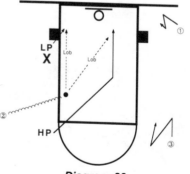

Diagram 22

In Diagram 22, Player 2 sees an opening and drives (using the long step move) to the free-throw line. As Player 2 drives, he looks for HP on the back-door cut, or for LP getting in low post offensive position for either a direct pass or a lob pass, or for a pass to either of the other two open perimeter players. Player 2 could also pull up for the jump shot or step-through moves. After a step-through move, if Player 2 is not open, he passes the ball to a teammate to keep the offense moving.

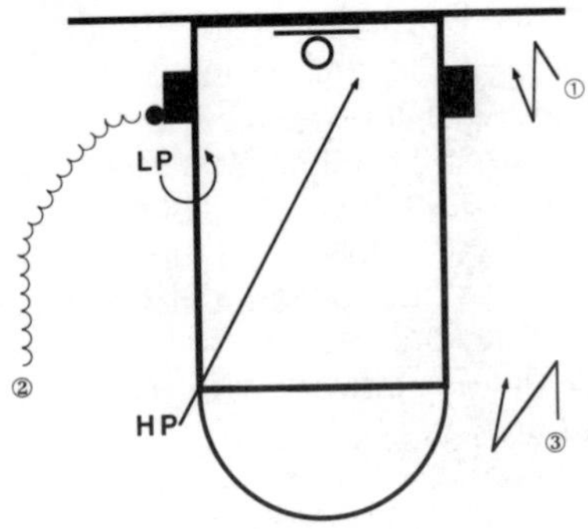

In Diagram 23, Player 2 drives to the baseline, using the crossover long step drive. As Player 2 drives, he looks for HP on the back door cut (lob pass), or for LP positioning for a close jump shot, should his man drop down to close off Player 2's drive. Player 2 may also find open a pass to one of the perimeter players or make a power play low or a pull-up jump shot or step-through move. If these scoring moves are not open, Player 2 will pass the ball back out to continue the offense.

Diagram 23

In Diagram 24, Player 2 sees no openings or passes inside and zips the ball back around to Player 3, who moves to the top of the circle and quickly continues the offense.

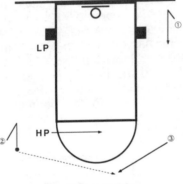

Diagram 24

Diagram 25 shows Player 3 continuing the offense that was originally shown in the Diagrams 15A and 15B.

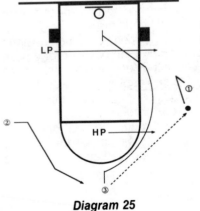

Diagram 25

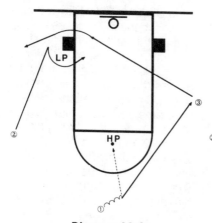

Diagram 26-A

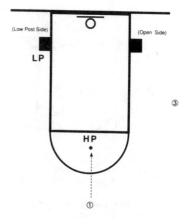

Diagram 26-B

In Diagram 26A, the point guard passes the ball to the high post man. Remember that Players 1, 2, and 3 are interchangeable, and they carry out their offensive assignments according to their position at the time the pass was made.

In Diagram 26B, we see that at the time the pass is made to the high post, the low post man will move to either one block or the other. Which block he chooses determines the movement of the other players.

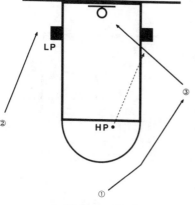

Diagram 26-C

In Diagram 26C the perimeter player (3) on the open side will cut to the basket for a possible lay-up because his area is clear. Player 2 will go to the baseline area and hold his position for a jump shot, while Player 1 moves to the open side to be available for a jump shot if his man stays on high post, or a safety outlet pass.

(Legend for Diagrams is in Appendix.)

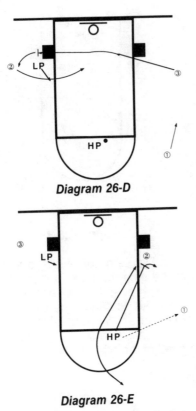

Diagram 26-D

Diagram 26-E

In Diagram 26D, Player 3 cuts around behind LP to see if he can get himself open for a short baseline jump shot. Player 2 times his cut so that he cuts across the top of LP just as Player 3 goes baseline, creating problems for the defense. LP steps up for the ball just as Player 2 cuts across. HP now has the option of passing to an open player or using his long step moves for a quick one-dribble pull-up short jump shot or step-through move. If HP is not open, and LP and Player 2 are not open on the block, then HP will pass (see Diagram 26E) to either 1 or 3. HP will pick down on Player 2, and 2 will pop out as the point man. At this point the offense will begin again. Note that either LP or HP can pop out to be the high post man as the offense continues.

In Diagram 27, the point guard 1 finds the low post man open and passes directly to him. The low post looks first for the high post to take a back-door cut, and then he looks for his own scoring opportunities. He will pass the ball back out to any of the perimeter players if the defensive team has dropped down to double team or help out on the low post.

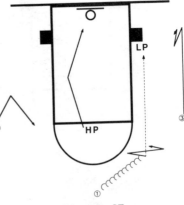

Diagram 27

VII. The Full Court Game

One of the most important parts of basketball is the full court game. Here all of the drills, individual offensive skills, and half court patterned scoring opportunities must be blended into a consistent method of bringing the ball up the floor and getting into an offensive scoring attack. The elements of the full court offense that we will discuss are the transition offense, tempo control, and attacking the press.

Transition Offense

Transition refers to the change from defense to offense or vice versa. Quickness is the most important factor to consider, and physical and mental conditioning are essential for each player to be able to use his skills and perform at his best in the transition game. If you have worked on the fundamentals outlined in this book and practiced the drills over and over, and if you and your teammates are willing to push yourselves physically, then the transition game is the place where you can excel. In this game, the step you take quicker than the opposing team or the one second head start taken in anticipation of a transition will make all the difference.

The first opportunities in transition come from the other team's mistakes which allow quick breaks from turnovers. If your team (on defense) is able to intercept a pass, pick up a loose ball, or a dribble that bounced too high, you should be able to quickly make the transition from defense to offense. We have already covered scoring from two-on-one and three-on-two breaks, which are all part of the transition offense. Now we will begin to think about the Quick Break which is a transition from half-court or full-court defense.

The Quick Break Using One Guard as the Primary Outlet

Diagram 28A shows the transition from defense triggered by a missed shot and rebound. The point guard (Player 1) moves to get open to receive the outlet pass. Player 2 moves to the middle of the court as a back-up outlet. Player 3 will sprint to the other end of the court opposite of Player 2 at about the free-throw line extended, where he will attempt to get open on the wing position.

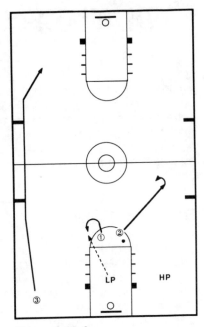

Diagram 28-A

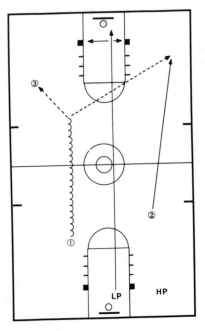

After the outlet pass is made to Player 1, the low post man will sprint to the other end of the floor and come to the ball side to get into offensive position on the block as a receiver (see Diagram 28B).

Diagram 28-B

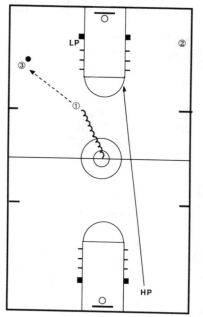

Diagram 28C shows the point guard passing the ball to the wing man (Player 3) and then following the pass to take a position at the top of the circle on the ball side. The ball can now be reversed to the weak side if Player 3 does not have scoring opportunities. The high post man is the trailer and sets up on the free-throw line away from the ball. Player 2 sets up on the wing opposite the ball.

Diagram 28-C

Diagram 28D shows the transition half court offensive set. Player 3 has all the regular one-on-one options available to drive or pass that we have covered in our skeleton and half-court offensive patterns. His first look is in to the low post.

In Diagram 28E Player 3 penetrates to the free-throw lane area. The other players move without the ball to get open, as we have previously described. (The same moves would also apply if Player 3 drove baseline.)

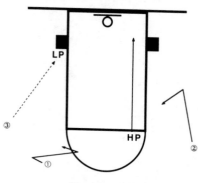

Diagram 28-D

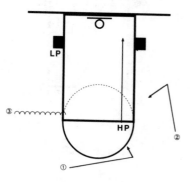

Diagram 28-E

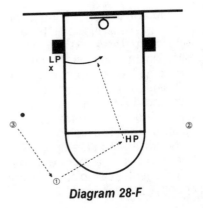

Diagram 28-F

Diagram 28F shows the ball being swung to the other side of the floor to take advantage of an opportunity for the low post. If the low post man is being fronted by his defender when the ball is on the wing, then the ball is reversed quickly so the low post can pin his man or step to the basket for an easy pass.

Diagram 28G shows a skip pass (Player 1 skips the pass to the high post man and passes directly to Player 2). Player 2 then tries to get the pass inside to the low post.

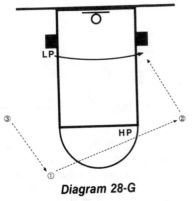

Diagram 28-G

Diagram 28H shows how the players move to get open when the ball is passed in to the low post.

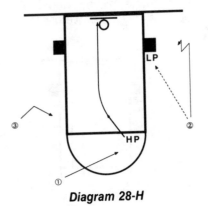

Diagram 28-H

Diagram 28I shows the ball being passed back to the point guard. We are now ready to get into the regular half-court offense.

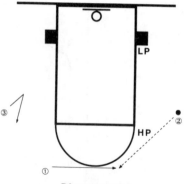

Diagram 28-I

The Quick Break Using Two Guards as the Primary Outlets

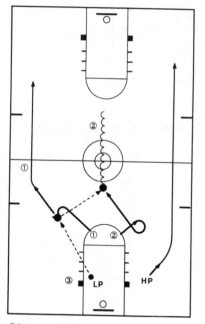

Diagram 29-A

Diagram 29A shows the use of both guards as primary outlets. As soon as the pass is made to guard 1 (or 2), the opposite guard (in this case 2) fills the middle lane. The first receiver (in this case 1) fills the closest lane while whichever player is nearest fills the opposite lane. Now we have a three-lane break with two trailers.

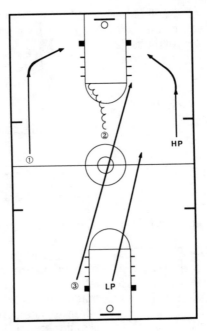

Diagram29-B

In Diagram 29B, the middle guard pulls slightly to the left side of the free-throw line and looks for the first trailer to cut to the basket.

In Diagram 29C, the player in the middle of the court (Player 2) could have passed to the first trailer (Player 3), passed to either of the wings, taken a jump shot himself, or hit the second trailer (Player 5) for either a jump shot or a power move to the basket.

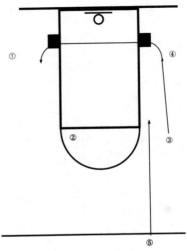

Diagram 29-C

Tempo Control

Tempo control is the ability of a team to speed up and slow down the pace many times during the course of a game. Coaches who are able to control the tempo have an advantage because their players can adjust more easily when a pressure situation forces a change in the tempo of the game.

A good quick break is necessary to be able to "up-tempo" the game. When you as a player are running the quick break, you are attempting to get a high percentage shot by beating the other players down the court. If you can get a high percentage shot after a minimum of passes that is excellent; however, the object is to gain a high percentage shot, not to see how quickly you can get off a shot. The players must be willing to continue passing the ball until the opportunity for a good shot comes.

Sometimes a high percentage shot will be available after only one or two passes. At other times a different tempo can be set by using an offense that pulls back out away from the basket and teases the defense by taking the ball inside, then bringing it out and attacking again. Tempo control can be attained in the man-to-man offense by using the continuity patterns we showed earlier, but it can be more clearly understood by the following contrast in two zone attacking offenses.

"Two Low" Offense

In Diagram 30A we illustrate a "quick hitting offense." Two post men are positioned low on the blocks, and the perimeter players pass the ball around the perimeter, always trying to get in an open shooting area. Once the shot goes up, the object is to gain a rebound and second shot.

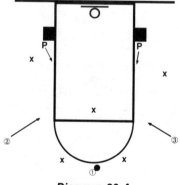

Diagram 30-A

In Diagram 30B, the post men make sure they are on opposite sides of the basket, and Players 2 and 3 rebound to the mid-area, while Player 1 is ready to get back on defense.

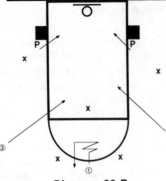

Diagram 30-B

The "Two Pick" Offense

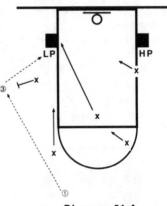

Diagram 31-A

In Diagram 31A Players 3 and 1 look inside to see if the low post man is open.

Diagram 31B shows Player 1 getting the pass back from Player 3. The low post man sets a pick for Player 1 to use for a drive.

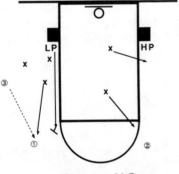

Diagram 31-B

Diagram 31C shows Player 1 driving off the pick to: 1) look for a shot, 2) pass to Player 2 whose man has moved in to help, 3) look for the high post who has stepped inside, or 4) look to see if Player 3 is open in the block area.

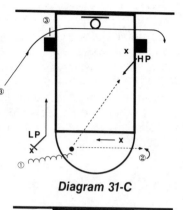

Diagram 31-C

Diagram 31D shows the team swinging the ball to Player 2 who either passes inside to the post or passes to Player 3 who has cut through to the corner. If Player 3 gets the ball, he looks to see if the post is open or if he (Player 3) is open for a jump shot.

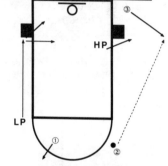

Diagram 31-D

Diagram 31E shows Player 3 passing out to Player 2, who will start the same offense back to the other side as the high post man sets a pick for Player 2.

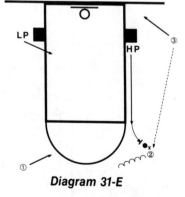

Diagram 31-E

Coaching Tips

In the "Two Pick" the tempo of the game is slowed, and the offense is teasing the defense by waiting until an excellent shot can be taken. Often in the "Two Low" a player will feel that he is open and will rush his shot. When a team is on, that is fine, but if too many shots are missed, it is time to change the tempo by switching to an offense such as the "Two Pick," where the players (because of the nature of the offense) will run the pattern longer, looking for an excellent high percentage shot.

Full Court Offense after Made Field Goals

The full court offense after made field goals is merely an extension of the quick break.

In Diagram 32, we see the players quickly make the transition from defense to offense with the high post man throwing the ball in to the point guard while the other players sprint down court.

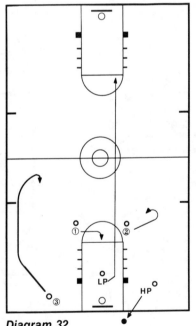

Diagram 32

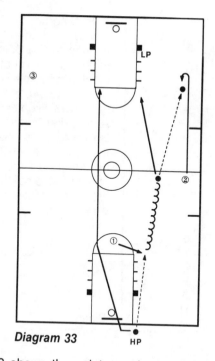

Diagram 33

Diagram 33 shows the point guard moving the ball to the wing position (either Player 2 or 3) and the low post man moving to the ball side with the high post pulling up as the trailer.

Attacking the Press

Attacking the press should be as similar as possible to your regular full court offense. If you have to set up differently to attack the press, it will give an advantage to the defensive team, which will have more time to be effective. Also, your quick breaks will be vulnerable because anyone will be able to slow them down by simply going to a press.

Youth League Basketball

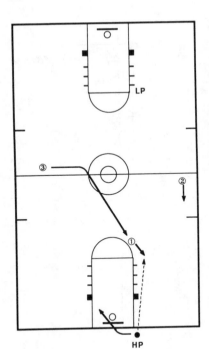

In Diagram 34 the high post man again brings the ball out of bounds to the point guard with the 2 and 3 men at half court to break back as needed. When the high post sees there is a press, he delays slightly at the defensive basket for two purposes: (1) He could be a passer to swing the ball to the weak side, and (2) he could be a defensive safety should the other team succeed with their press and come up with the ball.

Diagram 34

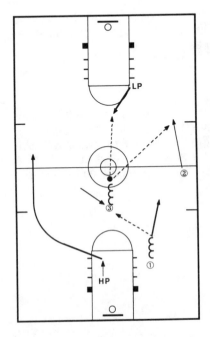

In Diagram 35 the point guard (1) pases to Player 3, who breaks up into the middle of the press. Player 3 then looks for the low post man who has popped up to be a receiver at the top of the circle. Player 2 and the high post man also cut.

Diagram 35

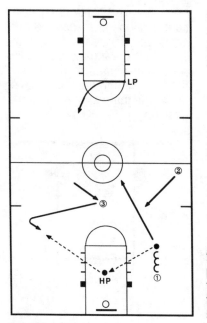

Diagram 36-A

In Diagram 36A, we assume that Player 3 was not open. The point guard reverses the ball to the high post, who zips the pass to Player 3 who has cut to the off side to get open. After Player 3 receives the ball, he immediately attempts to get the ball back to the point guard, who should be open as he cuts through the mid-court area (Diagram 36B). Also, Player 3 may look down court to see if the low post is open or back to Player 2 as an outlet.

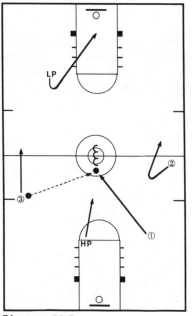

Diagram 36-B

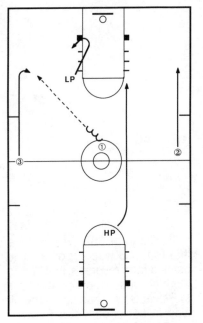

Diagrams 37 and 38 show the continuation down court as the point guard pushes to get the ball to either wing 2 or 3. The low post man comes to the side of the ball with the high post pulling up for the jump shot in the trailer position.

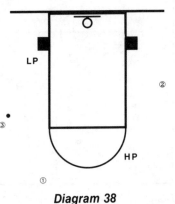

Diagram 37   **Diagram 38**

Coaching Tip

Again, there are a great number of methods that can be devised to attack the press successfully, but it is very important that your press attack incorporate bringing the ball in the same way and using the same strategies that are employed in the quick break.

VIII. Defense

Defensive Drills

Here are some defensive drills that help a player and a team develop the skills needed to play what has been called a pressurized man-to-man defense with help tendencies on the offside." Drills that will help individual players' skills and drills that will help teams develop the teamwork necessary for an overall defensive strategy will be presented.

8-1 Defensive Position
Body balanced with weight equally distributed. Feet shoulder's width apart, one slightly ahead of other; knees flexed; head up and eyes focused ahead.

One good way to understand the difference between pressure on the ball side and help on the offside or weak side is shown in the following diagram:

Player 1 has the basketball. His man keeps pressure on him, containing him with his feet squared away directly between the offensive player and the basket, also keeping his hands in the passing lanes to discourage a pass or a shot.

Player 2 is the offside guard. The defense is in a helping position so that he can see both his man and the ball, and he keeps his hands in the open passing lanes to discourage the offensive Player 1 from passing into the inside scoring area (that is, to discourage a pass to Player 5 or to Player 4 should Player 4 move closer to the basket).

Player 3 is the post player. We always try to keep the ball out of the post by having the post defensive player side his man with one hand

75

in the passing lane and one foot behind the offensive post player so that the defense is never beaten on a back-door cut. Some teams use a high and a low post man, so a player must learn to defend both positions.

Player 4 is the offside or help side player. This is one of the most important positions on the floor. He must see his man and the ball at the same time. He is the interceptor for lob passes, should Player 3 or 5 cut back toward the basket. He also must watch to make sure that his own man does not break toward the ball to receive a pass. Should his man become a receiver, he must cover him and then tell the other players to loosen up their pressure on the ball because their help has been taken away. (See Diagram 39.)

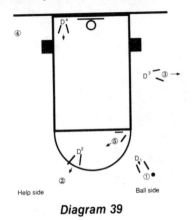

Diagram 39

Piece-of-the-Ball Drill

A and B pass the ball back and forth across the free-throw line or some similar area for 30 seconds while D tries to get his hands on the basketball. A and B must throw either a bounce pass or a direct pass no higher than D's outstretched fingertips. A and B must remain stationary, and they must not pass the ball over D's head. (See Diagram 40.)

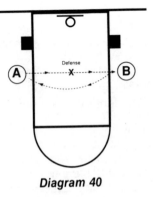

Diagram 40

Coaching Tip

Count the number of times each player gets his hand on a piece of the ball, and let all the other players know which player has the highest number of touches. Station groups of three around the gym and time the whole team at once.

One-on-One Full Court

This is a defensive sliding drill, when the offensive player dribbles in a zig zag, dribbling right, then correctly crossing over to dribbling left, continuing the zig zag pattern to the end of the court. You, the defensive player, keep your ball-side hand riding evenly to slightly above the ball with the opposite hand trailing slightly lower so that you can cut off the crossover dribble (See Diagram 41.)

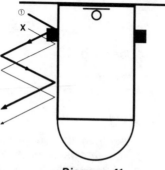

Diagram 41

If a dribbler attempts to reverse the ball (turns his tail to you), immediately take a step backward, so that he can't beat you to the basket. As he comes face to face, regain normal defensive posture of your ball-side hand even with or higher than the ball, and your opposite hand lower than the ball to cut off the crossover dribble.

Coaching Tip

The defensive player's head should be just slightly to the ball side of the center of the offensive player's body.

Contesting and Help

Player D1 is in position to contest the pass from the ball-side guard while D2 is in the help position, should the ball be lobbed over to O1 in a back-door cut. When the ball is passed back around to horn, D2 comes out to contest the pass to his man, and D1 moves into helping position. (See Diagrams 42A & B.)

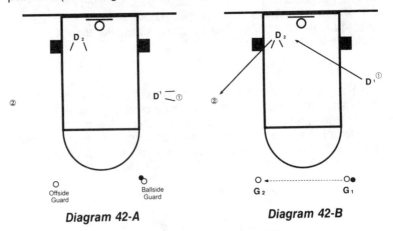

| Diagram 42-A | Diagram 42-B |

Coaching Tip

This drill should be done with great intensity. To insure the intensity of the drill, always use your two most competitive athletes first.

Contesting to Containing

Contesting a pass means trying to keep your opponent from receiving the ball. The coach throws a pass to O. When D1's opponent receives the ball, D1 establishes a good one-on-one defensive position so that he can have a hand up to deter the outside shot. He also squares his feet and body so that he is in a position to contain his man so that O1 cannot drive directly to the basket. (See Diagram 43A & B.)

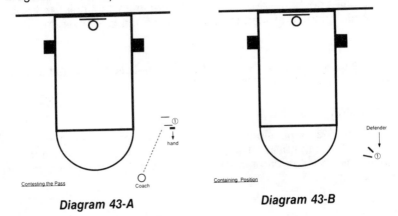

| Diagram 43-A | Diagram 43-B |

Coaching Tip

This is also a good opportunity for O to work on his offensive moves.

Drop to the Ball and Recover

When D1 is in containing position and the ball is passed inside, have D1 immediately drop on the ball, double teaming the post man so that he cannot drive to the middle of the floor, helping to prevent his shot, and attempting to keep his hands in the passing lanes of his own defensive opponent. When the ball is passed back outside, D1 immediately hustles to recover his defensive position so that he can keep O1 from getting a high percentage outside shot, while also containing him from driving directly toward the basket. (See Diagrams 44A & B.)

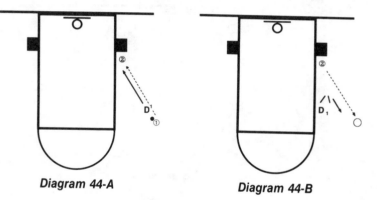

Diagram 44-A   **Diagram 44-B**

Coaching Tip

Dropping the ball and recovering quickly is one of the most demanding parts of man-to-man defense, but also one of the most important.

Playing the Post

Always attempt to side the post man with your front foot almost in the passing lane, while the same-side is in the passing lane, contesting the pass. The back foot is behind the post man so that if the ball is caught, the defensive post man can quickly fight to recover a containing position where his body and feet are squared between his man and the basket, with his hand up to deter the shot. (See Diagrams 45A, B & C.)

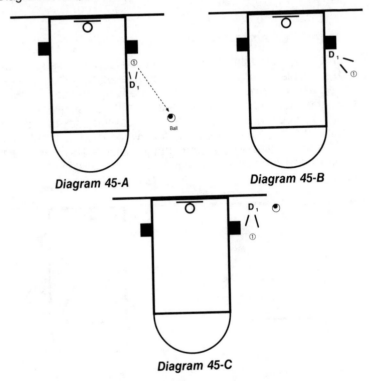

Diagram 45-A   **Diagram 45-B**

Diagram 45-C

Coaching Tip

On the baseline the post man would play the baseline side of the ball exactly as described above. *Always side the post man to the ball side.*

Rebounding

Rebounding is certainly one of the most important skills in basketball. Even though some players seem to have a knack for picking up rebounds, going for the ball each time a shot is taken seems to be the single most important factor in determining who will out-rebound whom.

Getting Position

While shots are taken from different offensive setups, the players should take the following steps: (1) Assume that each shot will be missed, (2) Get between your man and the basketball with your feet spread, elbows out, arms raised, and (3) As soon as you see where the ball is going, go for it, jumping with outstretched hands to grasp the ball firmly with both hands.

Coaching Tip

Make sure your player gets an advantage position, but the most important element to stress is to *Go for the rebound* after assuming that each shot will be missed.

8-2A Rebounding Position
Immediately after shot, move to position.

8-2B Rebounding Position
Block out your man from the backboard and keep your eyes on the ball.

8-2C Rebounding Position
Explode up for the ball, extending body fully.

Beating Your Man To The Basketball

As the offensive man cuts to the ball, you front him, staying between him and the basketball until he becomes a post man. Then follow the same principles as siding the post and recovering if your man receives the ball. (See Diagrams 46A & B.)

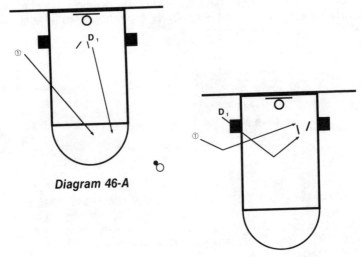

Diagram 46-A

Diagram 46-B

Coaching Tip

If a shot should go up from the outside during this struggle to keep the inside player from catching the ball, the defensive player must work to gain a rebounding position that puts him closest to the ball, and then go for the rebound.

Half-Court Man-to-Man Defense

Even though each player is assigned to guard a particular offensive player, there are also other responsibilities in the full defensive scheme. The half-court man-to-man defense fuses all the drills that we have worked on into a continuous process of containing the player with the ball (in this case Player 1). The onside player (in this case 3 and 5) contests the pass to his opponent, and the offside player (2 and 4) helps. (See Diagram 47.)

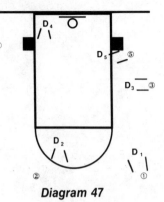

Diagram 47

Coaching Tip

The key is to figure what your opponents' offense is trying to do to free an offensive player for a shot, and then prevent them from running that particular play. Cut off a key pass, get in the pathway of a key player's cut, or force a player to dribble in the direction opposite to where he wants to go.

(Legend for Diagrams is in Appendix.)

IX. A Coach's Responsibilities

Team Morale

You cannot completely control the attitudes of each individual player, but you do have a responsibility for setting the pace and the example for the team. Even if you are a beginning coach and are not as yet familiar with teaching the skills in this book and developing coaching strategies, you can still be a positive leader and role model for your players, and you can work to provide a positive experience for each child. As you prepare to coach, consider the following:

Positive Criticism

For young players to achieve success in any endeavor, they need to be confident that their efforts will be met with affirmation. Particularly with very young players, negative and impatient remarks can be very destructive to both spirit and motivation. Most children will work much harder and achieve much more if they are met with enthusiastic support and helpful criticism.

Playing Time

Most leagues have rules about the amount of time that each player must play in each game. If the teams have been matched fairly, then each coach should understand that allowing everyone plenty of playing time is crucial both to the development of players and to team morale. The coach must try to win, and to be successful, he or she must foster a spirit of fun and co-operation.

Team Concept

Allowing players time to feed back after each practice and game is a positive way to foster a team concept. Ask, "What did we do well today?" Or, "What do we need to work on at our next practice?" Be sure to applaud the unselfish players on the team as well as the stars. Try to develop leaders within the team ranks.

Discipline and Motivation

Most young people respond well to straightforward and positive leadership. Set expectations at the beginning of each season and practice in a way that lets the players know that you are interested in helping them learn and win and have fun. Youthful players do not respond well to intimidation or to leaders who are only interested in themselves. Be enthusiastic, understanding, and sensitive to individual needs, and you will meet some very crucial emotional needs of your players as well as make friends for life.

Liability

Because they have volunteered their time, many coaches never realize that they are responsible for the welfare of the youngsters they coach. The feeling is that because they are donating their time they are not really held accountable. Nothing could be further from the truth.

Morally, the volunteer coach is held responsible for any psychological damage he may cause youngsters. In a sense, parents are depending on him or her to see that proper attitudes are instilled in their youngsters' minds. Volunteers who agree to coach also agree to be responsible for the safety of the young people they coach. If proven negligent, coaches may be held liable for physical harm incurred by players in their charge.

Included in this section are some areas that every conscientious coach should be informed about before beginning work as a volunteer.

Physical Examinations

Every youngster participating on the team should have a physical examination with written approval from a medical doctor stating that he is physically fit to participate in athletic competition. **Don't risk the chance of serious injury because you didn't take the time to see whether the player was medically fit!**

Safe Equipment

The old saying, "You get what you pay for," applies here. What you might get, perhaps, are broken collarbones and sprained ankles if the equipment purchased is not of good quality.

Good Facilities

Poor or inadequate facilities can result in a multitude of injuries. Some causes: ruts or holes in the field of play, rocks on the infield of a ball diamond, slippery floors in gyms, inadequate padding under the basket in basketball. All a good coach has to do is look around and say to himself, "Do things look safe?" If they do, he has no problems.

Provide Plenty of Liquids

Contrary to the belief held by many old-timers, water is not only good to drink during practice sessions, it will help prevent heat exhaustion and dehydration.

In fact, medical research indicates that during exercise it is necessary to replace water loss (perspiration) hour by hour. Also, on hot days athletes should drink plenty of water prior to their practice or game. Carbonated beverages or those that contain sugar are not recommended.

How Many Games to Play

Volunteer coaches sometimes get so wrapped up in the thrill of coaching (especially if it's a winning team) that they schedule extra games for the kids—some areas of the country have reported as many as eighty basketball games during one season. It is both unrealistic and unhealthy for a youngster to be involved in so many games per season. Why? Here are a few reasons.

1. The physical strain of too many basketball games can drastically affect the overall system of an adolescent.

2. The psychological strain of winning and losing can take its toll on a youngster's emotional growth.

3. Young people also have home, school, and social responsibilities which compete for their time and can be adversely affected by overemphasis on competitive sports. The average number of high school basketball games played during a season in the United States is twenty. This established number is based on concern for the overall development of the individual. If school systems feel it is important to limit the number of games, so too should the volunteer youth coach.

Listed below are the recommended numbers of scheduled games for various age levels per season:

    9 to 10 year olds — 12 games
    11 to 12 year olds — 14 games
    13 to 14 year olds — 16 games

Know the Rules

Agreeing to coach means you also agree to know the rules. A coach who "thinks" he knows the rules because he watches television on the weekends is only fooling himself. There is a big difference between pro rules and high school or youth league rules. Many games have been lost simply because a coach did not take the time to learn the difference.

Care of Athletic Injuries

Did you ever stop to think that your actions in case of an injury could, in the most extreme case, save an individual's life or, in the mildest case, have your player back in action in a matter of minutes? Think about it—it's true.

The care of athletic injuries is a subject too vast and complicated to be covered here. Our purpose in this publication is simply to inform you, the volunteer coach, as to: (1) the practical equipment you should have on hand at all times, (2) the most common injuries in youth basketball and (3) the immediate first-aid steps to follow in case one of these injuries occurs.

Practical Needs

1. **Most sporting goods stores carry regular coach's first-aid kits.** As a check list, however, all coach's first-aid kits should always contain:
   • Adhesive tape (several different sizes for several purposes)
   • Ammonia caps for dizziness
   • Antiseptic solution (betadine)
   • Aspirin for simple headaches
   • Plastic bottles for carrying water
   • Cold packs
   • Elastic wraps of various sizes
   • ads
   • Soap
   • Scissors

- Tongue depressors
- Eyewash solution with an eyewash glass

2. Tape the telephone number of the nearest ambulance service inside the first-aid kit. Always know where the closest available phone is at every game or practice site. Also tape a quarter to the inside of the first-aid kit, in case the closest phone is a pay phone.

3. Whenever possible have a physician or nurse present. A check with the players at the beginning of the season is an easy way to determine whether any parents are doctors or nurses. If any of them are, call and ask them for help during the season. They often are quite willing to help.

The Basic Approach to First Aid

1. Always remain calm. It's not easy, because the first sight of an injury can be upsetting. Nevertheless, helping to keep the injured player calm can sometimes be the best first aid you can render. This can only be accomplished if you remain calm yourself.

2. Never assume the role of a physician. The old saying, "It is better to be safe than sorry," is one that intelligent volunteer coaches will heed. Whenever there is any doubt, refer to a physician.

3. Never move a player who has a serious injury. This includes not sitting him up.

4. Use good judgment by stopping to think.

5. Never continue play of the game when a serious injury occurs.

Common Injuries and Immediate First-Aid Procedures

1. *Nosebleed*
Have the player sit and apply cold to nose (ice cubes or cold cloth) while pinching pressure at the bridge of the nostril that is bleeding

2. *Scrapes and burns*
Wash with cleansing solution that can be found in most coach's first-aid kits. Cover with clean gauze.

3. *Unconscious player*
Do not move the player. Have one of your assistants call for an ambulance. Stay with the injured player and check to make sure that the breathing passages are clear.

4. *Back injury*
If the pain is severe and numbness in the legs results, immediately send for an ambulance. Do not attempt to move the injured player.

5. Neck injury

As with any back injury, do not attempt to move or sit the player up if the pain is severe, and especially if there is numbness or lack of feeling. Keep the injured player calm. Many times a head injury can be a neck injury; therefore, treat it accordingly.

6. Heat

Heat prostration is the inability of the human body to cool itself rapidly enough to keep up with the heat gained through exercise. In hot to humid weather the body cannot sweat and dissipate heat effectively. If an available source of water to replenish sweat is lacking, the problem is compounded.

Treatment should be directed at the immediate cooling of the body. Keep the player flat and move him into a shaded, cool and well-ventilated area. If the player is responsive, small amounts of water may be given until an ambulance arrives.

7. Blister

A fluid accumulation between layers of skin caused by friction. If the blister is intact, use a sterile needle to make a small hole at the base of the blister. The fluid will drain out, and the blister's toughened skin serves as a protective covering for the sensitive area beneath. If the blister is broken, remove the dead skin with sterile scissors and soak the area in warm soapy water. Apply a sterile dressing coated with some antibiotic ointment.

8. Abrasion

A rubbing off of skin caused by sliding or falling. Wash the wound with unperfumed soap and water in order to remove any foreign matter. Continue to wash it twice a day to keep it clean. Also keep the wound exposed to the air as much as possible in order to promote healing.

9. Laceration

Jagged tearing of the skin and/or tissue. Any cut with marked bleeding should be seen by a physician. Direct pressure will almost always stop bleeding. Clean the wound lengthwise with unperfumed soap and water and cover it with a sterile dressing. Suturing may be necessary, especially if the wound is deep or if the cut is over a joint or on the foot or hand.

10. Bruise

A bruise caused by a blow to the body resulting in mild to severe pain with or without swelling. Apply ice to the area, then compress with an elastic wrap and elevate. Use ice if there is no pain when walking, jumping, or running. The bruise may last for a couple of weeks. If the athlete cannot walk or run or move his foot after 24 hours, medical attention is indicated. Emergency treatment should be sought if the area begins to swell immediately or severe pain occurs.

11. *Muscle Cramp*
A severe pulling or cramping of any muscle in the body. Stretch the muscle until the pain is gone. If the cramp is in the calf, push the foot against an immovable object until the pain goes away. If the pain is in the side of the abdomen, reach up as high as possible with your hand on the affected side until the pain disappears. If the pain persists, it is better to rest and apply ice packs to the muscle until the pain lessens.

12. *Strain*
The athlete will feel a sharp snapping sensation or pulling and will be able to point to the exact area of the strained muscle. The muscle will tighten and the athlete will slow down or be unable to continue participation in the game. Apply ice to the area, wrap with an elastic wrap, and elevate the injured part. No activity should be performed until there is absolutely no pain in the area. One does not "run off" these injuries! In other words, once a muscle is strained, the chances are that it will strain again if not properly treated.

13. *Sprained Ankle*
Swelling, tenderness, and bruising immediately around the front of the anklebone, coupled with inability to move up and down and/or sideways.

The treatment: ice, elastic wrap, elevation. To be on the safe side, we would suggest that an X-ray be taken to rule out the possibility of any serious ligament damage or a fracture. Athletes with any pain in the ankle should definitely not practice or play until the ankle is completely pain-free. NOTE: You should presume a fracture if your player is under 12 years old and has swelling, bruising, and tenderness over the ankle area.

14. *Testicular trauma*
A blow to the male genital region with or without difficulty in breathing. The player should be flat on his back with his knees bent and feet on the ground. Tell him to breathe through his nose and exhale through his mouth as if he were blowing a whistle. This should slow down the rapid breathing. He can resume activity when he is ready.

If he continues to have severe pain, you will have to check and see if there is any swelling in the scrotum and if both testicles are visible. If only one testicle is detected, the other may have been pushed up into the abdomen. This is an emergency situation that requires immediate treatment at a hospital. Ice should be applied to the scrotum if there is swelling in that area.

15. *Wind knocked out*
Difficulty in breathing resulting from a blow to the solar plexus. Treat with the same procedure as the testicular trauma case, using the nose-mouth breathing pattern.

16. *Head injury*

Make sure that the injured player is able to breathe easily, and have him professionally removed to the hospital on a stretcher. If no stretcher is available, a door or a broad plank will serve that purpose. If a player is knocked unconscious but recovers quickly, he should not be allowed to return to the game or to further games until he has been thoroughly checked by a neurologist.

17. *Loss of Airway*

If a player is not breathing—from whatever cause—quick action is imperative. Make sure there is no obstruction in the mouth. With the player on his back, hold the head in both hands, one hand pressing the head backward and the other pushing the lower jaw upward and forward. Open your mouth wide, take a deep breath and seal your lips around the player's mouth while obstructing the nostrils with your cheek (or it may be necessary to have someone pinch the nostrils shut with his fingers). Blow steadily into the lungs for a few seconds and watch for the chest to rise, then remove your mouth. Inflations should be given at the rate of ten per minute. The first six inflations should be given as quickly as possible.

Should the player be in a state of spasm or convulsion so that his mouth cannot be opened, it will be necessary to inflate the lungs by the mouth-to-nose method. Work from the side of the player. Make sure his head is extended. Open your mouth wide, take a deep breath and seal your lips widely on the player's nostrils. Close the mouth by placing your thumb on the lower lip. If the head is not sufficiently extended, the soft palate will allow inflation through the nose but may prevent expiration. If his happens, part the player's lips with your thumb after each inflation.

After about 10 to 12 breaths, properly given, look for improvement in face and lip color, which should become more pink and less bluish. If there is no such improvement, quickly feel for the pulse at the side of the neck and at the wrist and listen carefully with your ear pressed to the bare chest over the heart. Look at the eyes, and note the size of the pupils. If no heartbeat can be felt or heard and the pupils are dilated (large) or beginning to dilate, external cardiac massage should be started immediately.

While receiving mouth-to-mouth resuscitation, the player should be lying on his back. Locate the lower half of the sternum or breastbone and place the ball of your hand on it, with the second hand covering the first. After each inflation of the lungs, apply six to eight sharp presses at the rate of one per second. The idea is to depress the sternum about one inch with no more force than necessary. Remember that for younger players less force will be needed than for adults.

When the heart starts beating, external cardiac massage should stop, but respiratory resuscitation should be continued until normal breathing is re-established.

18. *Serious Bleeding*

Even severe bleeding, such as occurs when a large artery in a limb is damaged, can almost always be stopped by direct pressure with the thumbs and fingers over that part of the wound from which the blood is coming. This should be done **immediately.** Sterile pads should be applied if possible, but don't wait while someone looks around for them. Better an infected wound than a dead player.

If the bleeding does not stop with direct pressure, a tourniquet should be applied without further delay. This may be a narrow folded triangular bandage or sling, a large folded handkerchief, a strip of strong cloth, an elastic belt or suspenders or a piece of rope or rubber tubing. It is applied above the wound around the upper arm or thigh, tightly enough to compress the main artery and control the bleeding. The player should be taken to a hospital as quickly as possible.

Important Notice On First Aid

To be sure of proper first-aid application, contact your local first-aid or Red Cross offices for the most up-to-date publications.

X. Practice Procedures

Two-Hour Practice

2:45		Stretching exercises and rope jumping	
3:00	(10 min.)	Dribbling Passing Lay-ups 3-on-1 2-on-1	(During this 10-minute period select different drills for each practice in order to teach the basic skills.)
3:10	(10 min.)	Shooting skills and 1-on-1 moves	
3:20	(10 min.)	Defensive drills	
3:30	(15 min.)	Skeleton offense or Skeleton defense	
3:45	(15 min.)	Half court offense vs. man to man and half-court defense to full court offense and defense	
4:00	(3 min.)	Break	
4:03		Game situation	
4:20	(5 min.)	Chalk talk--Making constructive corrections	
4:25		Game situation	
4:45	(7 min.)	Free throws	
4:52	(8 min.)	Clock Situation*	

One-Hour Practice

2:45		Stretching exercises and jumping rope
3:00	(8 min.)	Dribbling Passing Lay-ups 3-on-1 2-on-1
3:08	(7 min.)	Shooting skills and 1-on-1 moves

3:15   (5 min.)   Defensive Drills
3:20   (12 min.)   Half-court offense and defense
3:32   (8 min.)   Full court offense and defense
3:40   Game situation

*Sample clock situations:
One minute to go and one point ahead.
One minute to go and one point behind.
Six seconds to go, one point behind, ball in bounds at opposite end of floor.

XI. A Player's Responsibilities

To the Coach

Your coach is a person who gives many hours of his time just for you, hoping you will learn many of the things which will help you become a good basketball player. In basketball the name of the game is learning to do your best because many times the difference between doing well and doing your best means a loss or a win for your team. Therefore, at all times it is your responsibility to give your coach your very best effort. That means paying close attention to his instructions and obeying the rules he has set up.

In basketball, there can be many things to learn. For instance, every play the coach designs requires you to do a special job. It may be making a pick, screening for a fellow player or positioning yourself for a rebound. In any case, your coach has designed a play which he feels will score a basket for your team. It will be your responsibility to know your job and be ready to perform it at the right instant. The end result might spell success for your team.

To the Referee

Every competitive game has to have someone to enforce the rules, and the purpose of rules is to make playing the game fair for all.

A referee does not have an easy job because he must constantly make accurate decisions on the play of the game. The basketball referee wants to do as good a job as he can to make the game fair for both teams and he needs your help to do this job. Therefore, basketball players have the responsibility of listening and cooperating with the referees of the game at all times. Most important, since he has the authority to make these decisions, the referee has the right to the respect, not the abuse, of players, coach and spectators.

The following code of behavior might help to make youth basketball the good experience it should be.

B—Be understanding when a referee makes a decision.

A—Accepting the decisions of the referee shows you are growing up.

S—Show the referee the same respect you'd want if you had the job.

K—Keep your emotions under control.

E—Don't embarrass your coach and team by abusing the referee.

T—The referee has a thankless task—don't make it any harder for him.

B—It is a rare occasion when a bad call by the referee is the reason a team loses the game.

A—Attempt to understand why the referee made a call—even when you disagree.

L—Remember, the referees carry a heavy load when it comes to making instant decisions.

L—Don't be a double loser because you blame the referee instead of your own failures when your team loses a game.

To Yourself

Playing basketball means you must make certain sacrifices. It means you must attend practices called by your coach. You must eat properly and get enough hours of sleep, learn your assignments as best you can on all plays and work hard at all that goes with being a winning basketball player. This includes being in top condition. It's important to keep yourself in good physical shape all year. You can't start playing basketball after months of little exercise and expect to progress very rapidly.

Exercising to stay in condition is not fun and should not be easy. To stay in shape, you must exercise rigorously and regularly; an off-again, on-again conditioning program will not be very helpful.

Building strength in your legs, arms, and upper body doesn't have to mean building bulging muscles. Most of the best players are not heavily muscled; rather, they are lean and firm looking. And players in top condition have hardly an ounce of extra fat. If you have developed the proper body strength, you will have muscles that ripple and bulge while you're playing—muscles to be proud of. But they will not stand out to an unusual extent when you aren't exerting them.

To develop good leg strength, you must do a lot of running. Just plain jogging, which is fine exercise for a nonathlete, isn't enough for the competitive player. You must combine jogging and sprinting.

Basketball has three speeds: slow, medium, and fast. All are important, because by varying them you can throw an opponent off guard. To do everything at one speed makes it easy for an opponent to keep pace with you. You must be able to surprise people with sudden spurts, changes of direction, and quick stops.

The key talent is acceleration—the ability to take off suddenly and at top speed. We often use the word *explode* to describe this movement. You must be able to explode into an opening to receive a pass, or explode past a defender to drive to the basket. And on defense, you must be able to accelerate whenever your opponent does, to keep up with him.

You have to be in top shape so that you can use any type of running speed at any point in the game. No tiring out at the end—this gives your opponents a chance to overcome you. You want to be able to keep pressure on them, not the other way around.

Try this simple running program to get in shape: Jog away from your home for about fifteen minutes, running steadily the whole way. Stop, rest for a few minutes, and catch your breath. On the way home, alternate jogging and sprinting, using telephone poles or city blocks as markers. Sprint from one pole or street to the next; jog to the next one; sprint to the next one; and so on, all the way home. And when you sprint, really move—top speed all the way.

The arms also need special strengthening. For your grip and forearm strength, a simple exercise is to grasp a small ball (a tennis ball will do, if your hand is large enough) and grip it as tightly as you can for a count of ten. Relax, then grip again, and repeat ten times.

A more difficult exercise, but a good one, is fingertip push-ups. As the name implies, this means doing regular push-ups but not touching the floor with anything but your fingertips—and toes, of course! If you can't do this at the start of your conditioning program (most people can't), practice regular push-ups until your arms are strong enough to do fingertips.

Strength is not your only goal. You must also develop flexibility. Lack of flexibility is a major cause of injury among athletes. Many young players don't realize that you can't snap muscles suddenly into active, straining positions without damaging them. Muscle pulls, ankle sprains, and torn ligaments are the result.

Flexibility varies from player to player. Some people are naturally more flexible than others. Those who are less flexible must exercise more to develop limber muscles. This may mean practicing the following exercises each morning and evening, as well as at team practices.

Here are the exercises that you should practice every day. Remember, you can't do them once in a while. They will be absolutely no use to you that way. They must be done every day, because their effect is cumulative.

Flexibility Exercises

Feet and Ankles. Standing, roll your weight around on your ankles. Rock up on your toes, back on your heels, and outside and inside, feeling the weight lean on all surfaces of the ankles. Do each full roll to a slow count of ten. Repeat four times.

Achilles Tendon. The achilles tendon runs up the back of your ankle into your calf. Stand about a foot away from a wall. Put your hands on the wall and, keeping heels firmly on the ground, lean against the wall. Hold to a count of ten, feeling the tendon stretch; relax. Repeat four times.

Back of Thighs and Lower Back. Touch your toes and hold for a count of ten, bending your head in toward your knees and keeping heels firmly planted. Try to touch your head to your knees. Repeat four times.

Groin Area. Sit on the floor, bend your knees, and put the soles of your feet flat against each other. Hold your ankles and try to press your knees to the floor. Make sure you feel the stretching in the groin muscles. Hold your knees down to a count of ten; repeat four times.

Lower Back. Lie on your back and pull your knees up to your chin. Hold for a count of ten. Then pull your extended legs up straight, over your head, and touch your toes to the floor behind your head. Keep your legs straight and hold for a count of ten. Repeat each movement four times.

Arms. Extend your arms straight out to the sides and do ten circles forward, making a circle of about one foot in diameter and keeping arms as straight as possible. Then do ten backward arm circles.

Shoulders and Back. Reach your right hand back over your right shoulder, behind your head. Put your left hand behind your back and reach upward, between the shoulder blades. Try to grasp the right hand with the left, and hold for count of ten. Repeat with hands reversed. Most right-handed people have trouble doing the second version, because their left arms are usually so inactive. Keep working at it; you'll stretch out.

Neck. Roll your head all the way around, slowly, leaning as far as you can to the left, then back, then to the right, then forward. Be sure you feel the neck muscles stretching. Repeat four times, slowly.

Strength, speed, and flexibility—they add up to determine your total body output. It's hard work to develop a properly conditioned body, but the reward that comes when you meet the test in a game situation will be well worth the effort.

APPENDIX

Legend

X	-	Defender
O	-	Offense
ᴧᴧᴧᴧᴧᴧᴧᴧᴧ	-	Dribbling
——	-	Running
— —	-	Passing
P	-	Post
HP	-	High Post
LP	-	Low Post
↳	-	Working to get open for pass
\ /	-	Players Position
① ② ③	-	Offense Player

Glossary

AIR DRIBBLE: A play in which a player, after giving impetus to the ball once by throwing or tapping it, touches it again before it has touched the floor or has been touched by another player.

ASSIST: A pass to a teammate who scores directly or doesn't dribble more than twice before scoring.

BACKDOOR: An offensive maneuver in which a player cuts behind the defensive man and to the basket.

BALL CONTROL: Offensive strategy which prolongs possession of the ball by delaying shooting until the best possible situation develops. Also referred to as *deliberate offense, disciplined offense, stall ball, letting the air out of the ball.*

BALL HANDLER: Player who usually brings the ball from his team's backcourt to the front and initiates the attack. Also referred to as the *playmaker.*

BALL HAWK: Player who specializes in recovering loose balls.

BASE LINE: The end boundary line.

BASKET: An 18-inch ring which has a net attached to it. The object of the game is to put the ball through the basket. A team's "own" basket is the one into which team players try to throw the ball. The visiting team has the choice of baskets for the first half and the teams exchange baskets for the second half.

BENCH WARMER: A substitute.

BLOCKING: Personal contact which impedes the progress of an opponent who does not have the ball.

BOARDS: The backboards.

BONUS FREE THROW: A second free throw awarded to a shooter who is successful on his first attempt. This bonus is in effect for each common foul (except a player control foul) committed by a player whose team has committed six or more personal fouls in a half (or four or more in a half of a game played in quarters).

CHARGING: An individual foul involving contact resulting from a player with the ball moving his body or the ball into an opponent whose position is legal or whose path is already established. Contact caused by the momentum of a player who has passed or thrown for goal is a form of charging.

CONTROL: A player is in control when he is holding or dribbling a live ball. Team control exists when a live ball is being passed between members of a team.

CONVERSION: A successful free throw.

DEAD BALL: The ball is dead whenever a whistle is blown and after a field goal.

DISQUALIFIED PLAYER: A player who is removed from further participation in a game because he has committed his fifth personal foul, or for some other reason such as a flagrant foul.

DOUBLE DRIBBLE: A violation which occurs when a player continues dribbling after grasping the ball with both hands.

DRIBBLE: A play in which a player gives impetus to the ball one or more times, causing it to rebound from the floor so as to touch or regain possession of it.

DUNKING: Reaching above the rim to put the ball through the basket. Also called a *stuff shot.* Now a violation in NCAA and high school basketball.

FAST BREAK: Offensive strategy in which a team attempts to bring the ball into scoring position before the defense can set up. Also referred to as *run and gun, run and shoot* and *firehouse basketball.*

FOUL: A rules infraction for which the penalty is one or more free throws (except in the case of a double foul or a player control foul). Fouls consist of the following types:

    (a) Common Foul: A personal foul that is neither flagrant nor intentional nor committed against a player trying for a field goal nor part of a double or multiple foul.

    (b) Double Foul: Opponents commit simultaneous personal fouls against each other.

    (c) Flagrant Foul: A violent or savage unsportsmanlike act or non-contact vulgar or abusive display; not necessarily intentional.

    (d) Intentional Foul: One which the official judges to be designed or premeditated; not based on severity of the act.

(e) Multiple Foul: Two or more teammates commit simultaneous personal fouls against the same opponent (a "gang-up").

(f) Personal Foul: Involves contact with an opponent while the ball is alive or after the ball is in possession for a throw-in

(g) Player Control Foul: A common foul committed by a player while he or a teammate is in control of the ball.

(h) Team Foul: Any foul charged against the offending team. Two examples are making an illegal substitution and taking more than the legal number of time-outs.

(i) Technical Foul: Usually a non-contact foul by either a player or a non-player; occasionally a contact foul when the ball is dead.

(j) Unsportsmanlike Foul: Unfair, unethical or dishonorable conduct.

FREE THROW: Opportunity given to a player to score one point by an unimpeded shot from behind the free–throw line.

FRONT COURT; BACKCOURT: A team's front court is in the area of the court between the mid–court line and its basket. A team's backcourt is the rest of the court including the opponents' basket.

FULL COURT PRESS: Defense strategy in which a team guards the opposition closely in the backcourt as well as the front court. This device can employ both zone and man-to-man principles.

FUMBLE: Accidental loss of control of the ball by dropping it or permitting it to slip out of one's hands.

GIVE AND GO: Offensive strategy in which a player passes to a teammate and then cuts for the basket expecting a return pass.

GOAL: A ball that passes through the basket from above, the impetus having been legally given by any player.

GOAL TENDING: Touching the ball or the basket while the ball is on, above or within the opponent's basket.

HELD BALL: Occurs when two opponents grasp the ball so firmly that control cannot be maintained without undue roughness; a closely-guarded player (defensive player is no more than six feet away) holds the ball in his front court for five seconds; a team in its front court holds the ball for five seconds in an area enclosed by screening teammates; or a closely-guarded player dribbles or combines holding the ball and dribbling for five seconds within a few feet of a front court boundary intersection or in mid-court area.

HIGH POST: An offensive pivotman who stations himself in or near the outer half of the free-throw circle.

HOLDING: Personal contact with an opponent which interferes with his freedom of movement.

HOOP: The basket. Also called the *cage* or the *bucket.*

JUMP BALL: A method of putting the ball in play by tossing it up between two opponents in one of the three circles.

KEY: The free-throw lane and circle. Also called the *keyhole.*

KICKING THE BALL: A violation when done as a positive act. Accidental contact is not a violation.

LOW POST: An offensive maneuver in which the center stations himself just outside the free-throw lane close to the basket.

MAN-TO-MAN-DEFENSE: A defensive system in which each player guards an assigned individual.

OVERTIME: One or more extra periods to break a tie score.

PASS: Movement of the ball from one player to another, usually by throwing, bouncing or rolling along the floor.

PIVOT: Movement in which a player while holding the ball steps any number of times with the same foot, while the other foot (pivot foot) holds its point of contact with the floor.

ROLL: A movement by a screener after his teammate begins a drive off the screen. This is most effective if the defenders are forced to switch and can result in a basket for the man rolling.

SCREEN: A legal method of blocking a defender without causing contact. Screens can be set for moving players as well as stationary players and the player for whom the screen is set may or may not have the ball.

STRONG SIDE; WEAK SIDE: Side of the court where the ball is located; side of the court where the ball is not located.

THREE-SECOND LANE: That part of the free-throw lane between the free-throw line and the end line, including the lines bounding the area.

THREE-SECOND LANE VIOLATION: A player without the ball remaining for more than three seconds in the free-throw lane while his team is in possession of the ball. If he receives the ball in less than three seconds, he has three additional seconds to shoot or get out of the lane.

THROW-IN: A method of putting the ball in play from out-of-bounds.

TIE BALL: Occurs when two players of opposing teams place one or both hands firmly on the ball at the same time or when a player places one or both hands firmly on the ball already held by an opponent.

TIME LINE: The division line across mid-court, so called because the offensive team must advance the ball across it to the front court within ten seconds after gaining possession.

TRAVELING: Illegal progression in any direction while retaining possession of the ball in-bounds.

TURNOVER: Any loss of possession without a shot being taken.

TWO (OR THREE) ON ONE: Two (or three) players converging on the basket with only one defensive player to attempt to stop them.

VIOLATION: An infringement for which the ball is put in play from out-of-bounds. The penalties for all violations are taken at the sideline opposite to where the violation occurred.

ZONE DEFENSE: A defensive system in which players cover assigned court areas, rather than specific individuals.